CW01651582

# Let's Investigate

# Shapes 2

Written by Beryl Webber
& Jean Haigh

Published by Scholastic Publications,
Marlborough House, Holly Walk,
Leamington Spa, Warwickshire CV32 4LS.

Written by Beryl Webber and Jean Haigh
Edited by Jackie Cunningham-Craig
Sub-edited by Jane Morgan
Designed by Sue Limb
Illustrated by Roland Smith

Typeset by Studio Photoset, Leicester.
Artwork by Norfolk House Graphic
Designers Ltd, Lutterworth.
Printed in Great Britain by Pindar Print,
Scarborough.



ISBN 0 590 76021 1

Front and back cover: photographs by
Martyn Chillmaid, designed by Sue Limb.

# Contents

# About the series

Learning mathematics is a creative activity. This is as equally true for today's children as it was for Sir Isaac Newton. All learners explore the wealth of mathematical achievement, creatively putting their own stamp upon it and making it unique for them. For example the child who begins to have an awareness of infinity is personally recreating ideas that are part of our mathematical inheritance but which cannot be directly taught. The learner draws upon a wide variety of experiences and ultimately combines them to form a unique and personal notion of infinity.

But as we live in a social environment each individual needs to be able to communicate their own personal mathematics to a wider audience. Newton's mathematical principles would have been lost forever when he died had he not used some conventions to communicate his ideas. We all must follow conventions if we intend to share our mathematics with others.

'Mathematics is not just about number and shape, it can be said to happen whenever the mind classifies and creates structures.'
*(Notes on Mathematics in Primary Schools,* 1967)

This definition, written by the Association of Teachers of Mathematics, is as relevant today as it was more than 20 years ago. Investigative mathematics is a way of allowing children to become independent mathematical thinkers. Children who have the opportunity to experience mathematics in a variety of situations and who successfully face challenges are able to use their energy and enthusiasm to become creative mathematicians.

This philosophy is central to our thinking and underpins the *Let's Investigate* series. We hope that these books will provide useful resources and ideas for you to use in the classroom in order to give children some opportunities to explore the richness of mathematics. We have deliberately not structured the series to form a mathematics scheme or programme. It is a collection of ideas to be dipped into to support the children's learning. The activities are not necessarily arranged in any order of difficulty but attempt to open children's eyes to the awe and wonder of mathematics.

We both hope that you will find this series a useful and enjoyable classroom resource to share with your children.

Beryl Webber
Jean Haigh

# Introduction

Each topic in the series consists of three books: Book 1 which is aimed at approximately the six- to eight-year-old age range, Book 2 for the eight- to ten-year-old and Book 3 for children aged ten to twelve years. We feel that photocopiable pages are inappropriate for the very youngest children in school and so Book 1 is only suitable for children who have had some time to explore their classroom environment and to develop some basic manipulative skills.

All the activities are exploratory but range from completely open-ended tasks to those that have some parameters set. Most of the activities have ideas for further investigation which tend to be more wide ranging and cross curricular. The teacher's instructions in each book follow a similar format and the objectives of each activity are clearly stated. The photocopiable pages consist of large easy to handle drawings.

The photocopiable pages are resource sheets that can be used with individuals, pairs or groups of children. It is hoped that the ideas will be extended by the teacher and the pupils and that the resource sheets will be used and developed in other ways. The teacher's instructions include many questions which either the pupils or the teacher may raise. Children should be encouraged to pose and explore their own personal questions. Any statements made can be turned into questions. For example 'The sides are the same length' can be transformed into 'Are the sides the same length? How can I be sure?'

## Conceptual development

The underlying concepts for each activity are stated in the objectives. Each section has activities that contribute to the development of the particular concept in the title. The properties, dissections and fitting together of the shapes are explored. Ideas of regularity, parallel lines, angles, radius and symmetry are the major additional concepts developed. The section on triangles explores isosceles as well as equilateral triangles and the section on quadrilaterals explores rhombuses as well as squares and rectangles.

## Basic skills

The skills of cutting, folding, measuring, fitting together and turning are frequently used. Children will also need to be able to join dots to make a shape.

## Mathematical skills

- Hypothesising
- Tessellating
- Rotating
- Predicting
- Enlarging
- Measuring accurately

Opportunities are created for children to share ideas, discuss, appreciate aesthetics, follow instructions and to enjoy their mathematics.

## Materials

Most of the activities require pencils, coloured pencils, scissors, rulers and adhesive. The necessary materials have been kept deliberately to a minimum and all of them should be easily available. More materials are required for the 'Further activities'.

# Triangles

## Smaller and smaller

See photocopiable pages 9 and 10.

### Objective

To discover that all equilateral triangles are similar.

### Classroom development

Cut out the equilateral triangle from photocopiable page 9. Cut along the dotted line. Fold the remaining triangle into four smaller triangles to demonstrate that it is still an equilateral triangle.

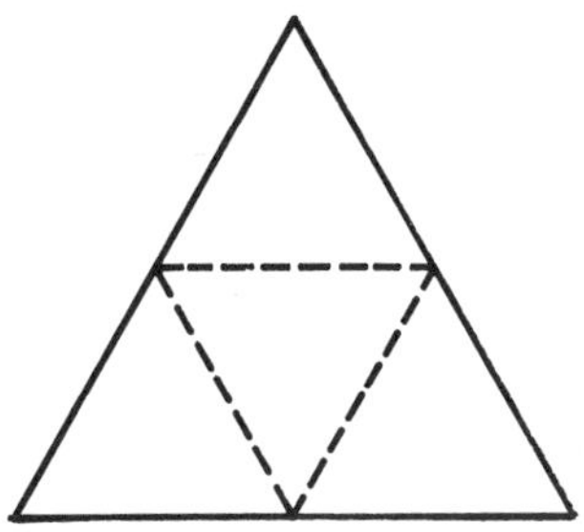

Match the triangle to the larger one on page 10 to show that they are the same size. Cut out this triangle. Cut along the dotted line. Fold it into four small triangles as before.

Repeat for the small triangle on page 10.

### Further activities

Using the largest equilateral triangle cut strips from the base and spread them out and mount them on to a piece of paper to make an expanded triangle. This shape appears to be an isosceles triangle.

Discuss the shape of the small triangle in the picture. Is it still equilateral?

## Making triangles

See photocopiable page 11.

### Objectives

To make equilateral, isosceles and scalene triangles. To identify their properties.

### Classroom development

The children will need three of each of the striped, dotted and plain strips (see page 11) and paper-fasteners.

Using the strips, how many different triangles can be made?

- dotted, dotted, dotted
- striped, striped, striped
- plain, plain, plain
- dotted, dotted, striped
- dotted, dotted, plain
- striped, striped, dotted
- striped, striped, plain
- plain, plain, dotted
- plain, plain, striped
- dotted, striped, plain.

Sort the triangles into sets. Can you sort them into three non-overlapping sets? The fact that equilateral triangles have three equal sides, isosceles triangles have two equal sides and scalene triangles have sides of different lengths can be explored here.

### Further activities

Get the children to make different triangles from a variety of materials such as matchsticks, pipe-cleaners, ribbon etc. These can be arranged as a display.

## Folding triangles

See photocopiable pages 12, 13 and 14.

### Objectives

To discover the lines of symmetry and properties of equilateral, isosceles and scalene triangles.

### Classroom development

Cut out the equilateral triangle on page 12. Use the measuring line to check the sides. Fold the triangle through the sun so that the edges meet. Notice that the two parts match. Open it up and draw a coloured line along the fold.

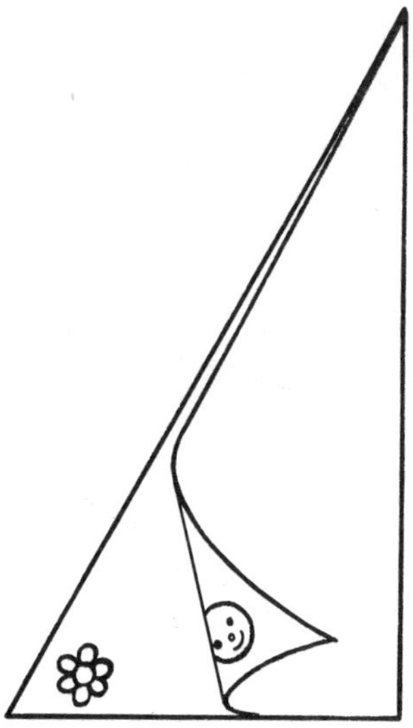

Repeat for the flower and the face but only colour the line if the two parts match. How many ways can an equilateral triangle be folded so that the parts match exactly?

Repeat this activity for the isosceles triangle on page 13 and the scalene triangle on page 14.

Take the equilateral triangle and cut along one of the coloured lines. Take one piece and check the sides. What do you notice? Use both parts to make a new triangle. Stick the new triangle down. What can you say about the new triangle compared to the original? Think about the lengths of the sides, the angles, the amount of space it takes up, the height and the symmetry? Repeat with the isosceles triangle.

Although there will be no coloured lines on the scalene triangle the activity could be attempted using a fold line. Can a new triangle be made? This could be tried by three different children using all three fold lines.

Draw the children's attention to their own discoveries. These could be shared with other members of the group, culminating in drawing together the group's discoveries.

# Fitting triangles

See photocopiable pages 15 and 16.

## Objectives

To discover the properties of the sides of equilateral, isosceles and scalene triangles.

## Classroom development

Cut out the two equilateral triangles on page 15 and put them together so that the sides match. Record what you have done. Try another way. How many ways can this be done?

Repeat for the isosceles and scalene triangles. Display the results.

Equilateral

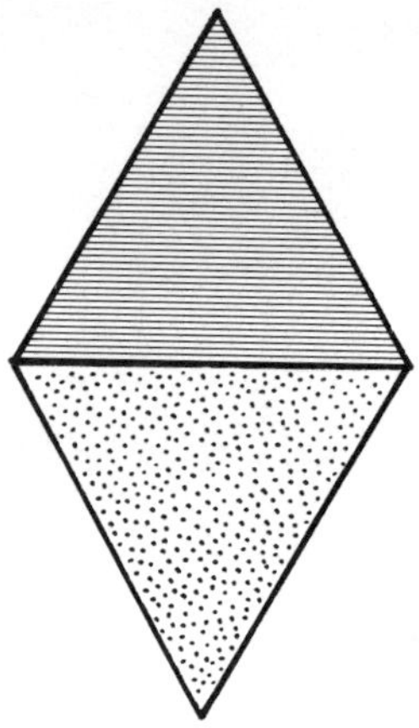

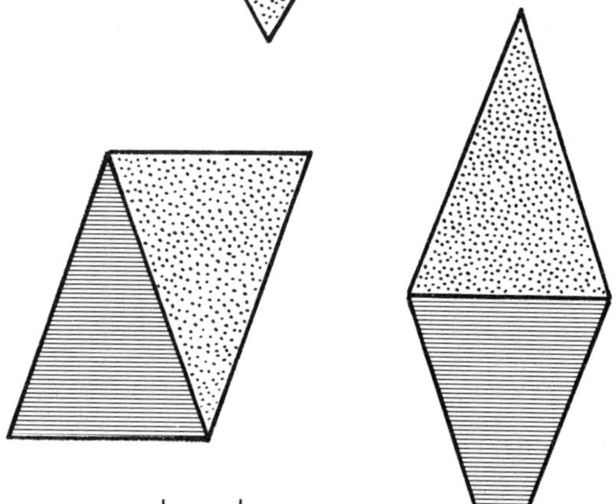

Isosceles

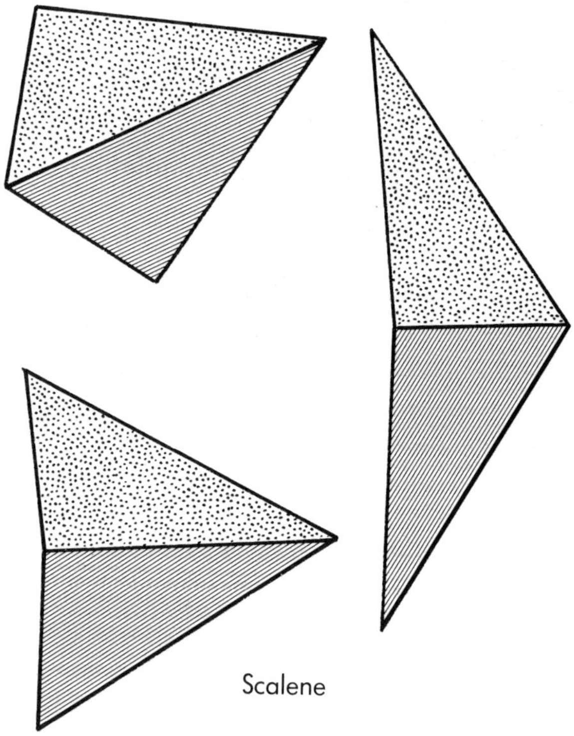

Scalene

## Further activities

Choose either of the dotted grids on page 16. Identify three dots and make a triangle. Cut it out and decide what type of triangle you have made. Consideration will have to be given to the strategies for making this decision. Why do different types of triangle come from different types of dotted grids?

# Smaller and smaller

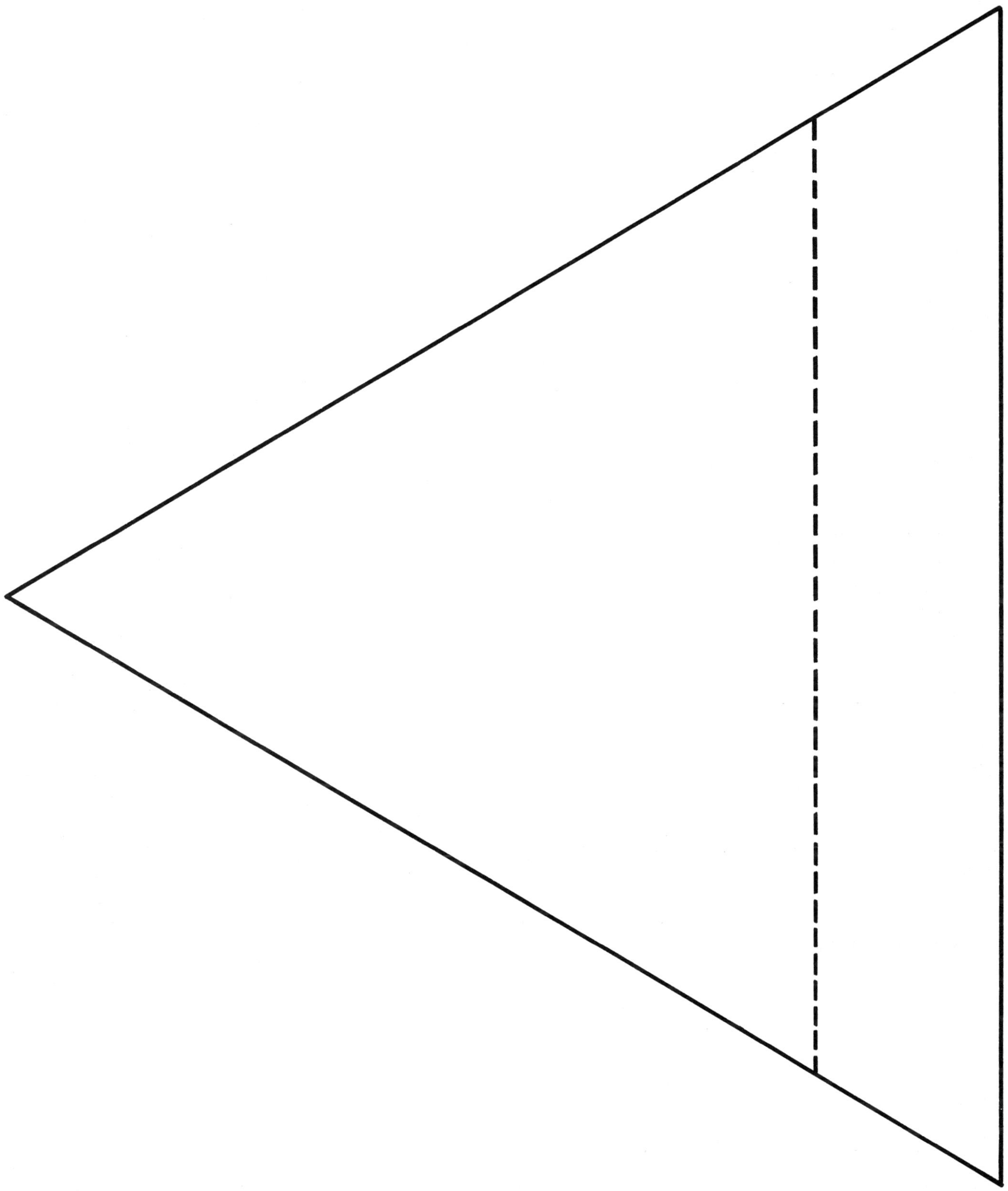

# Smaller and smaller

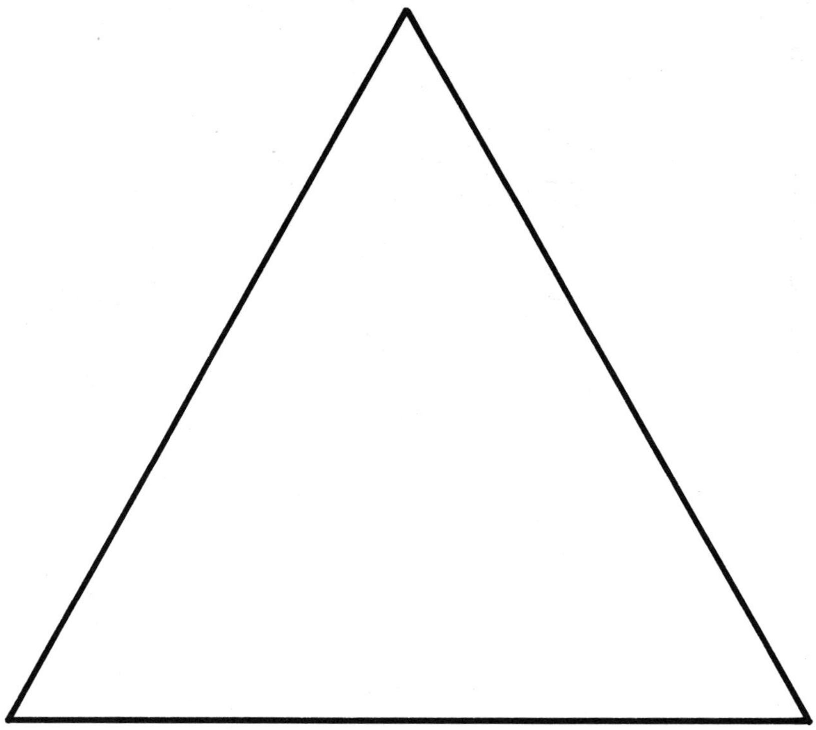

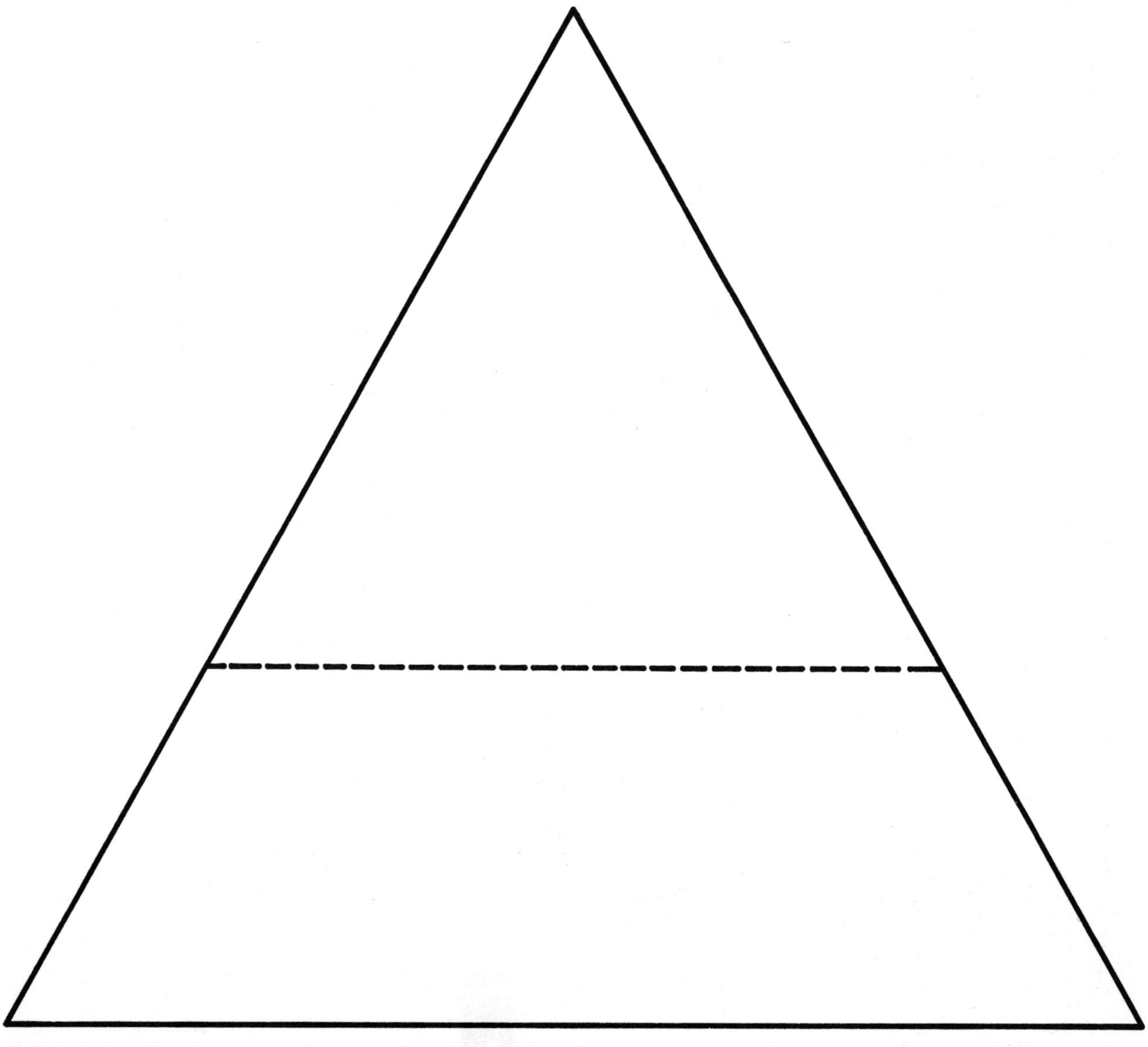

# Making triangles

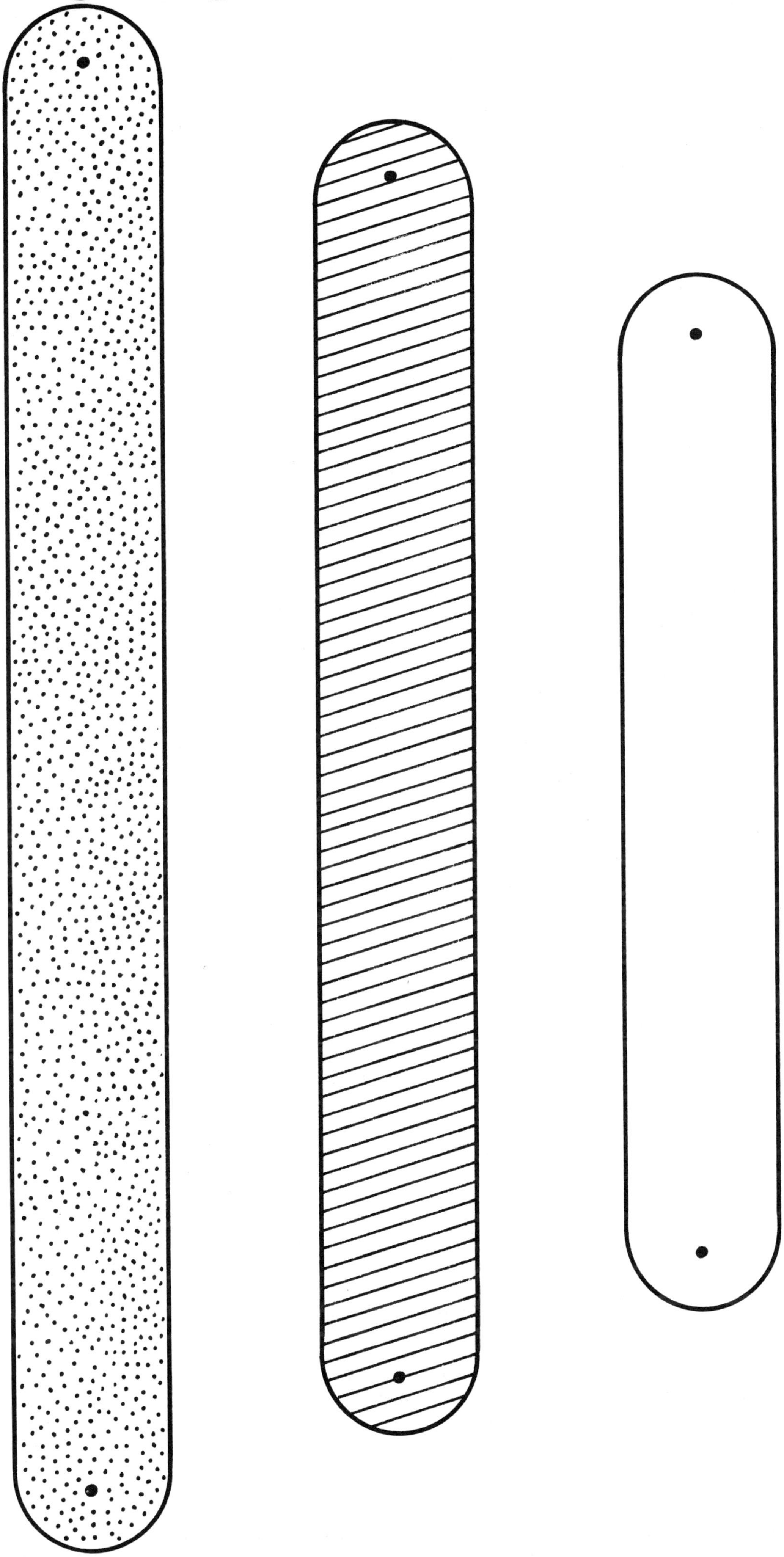

# Folding triangles

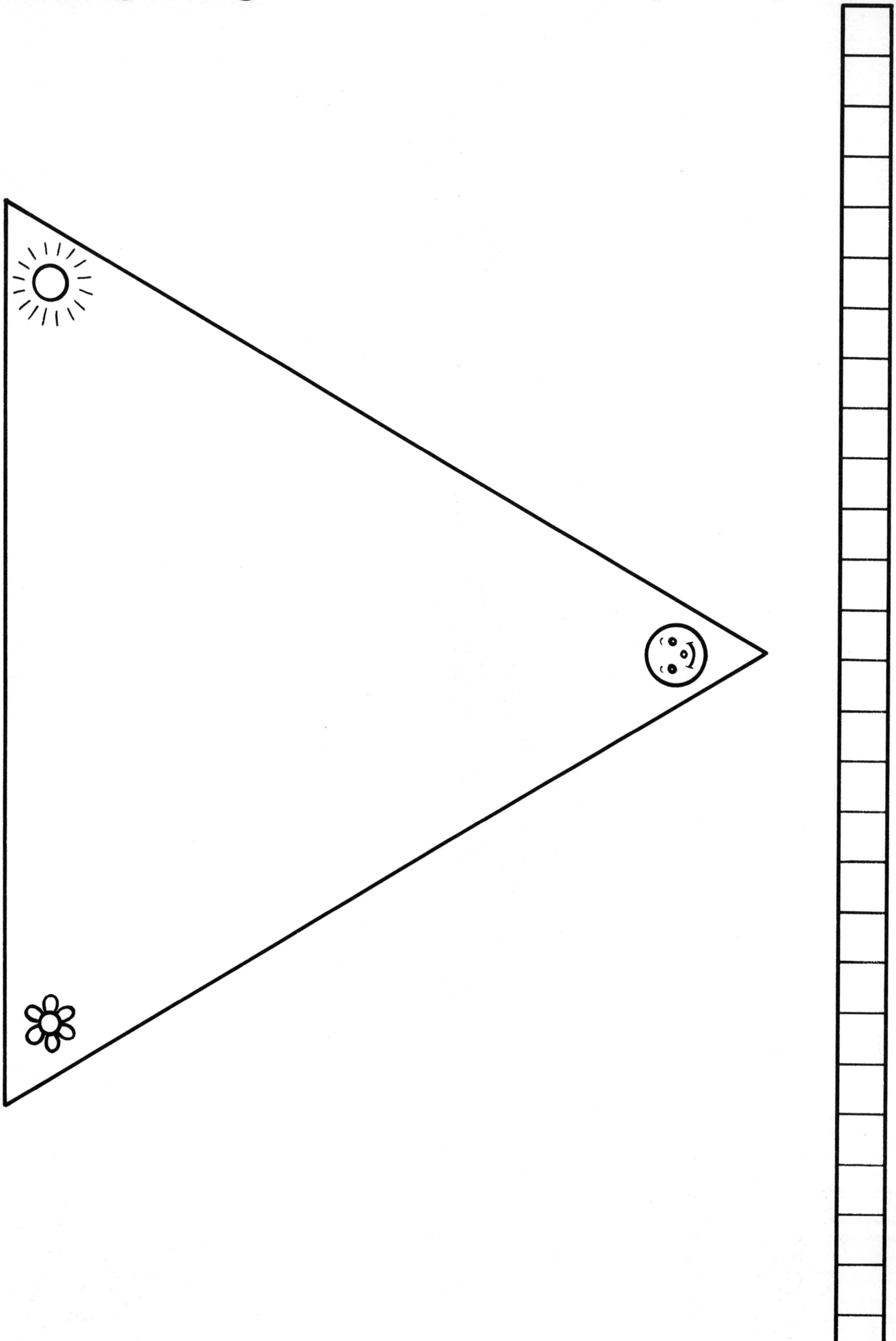

# Folding triangles

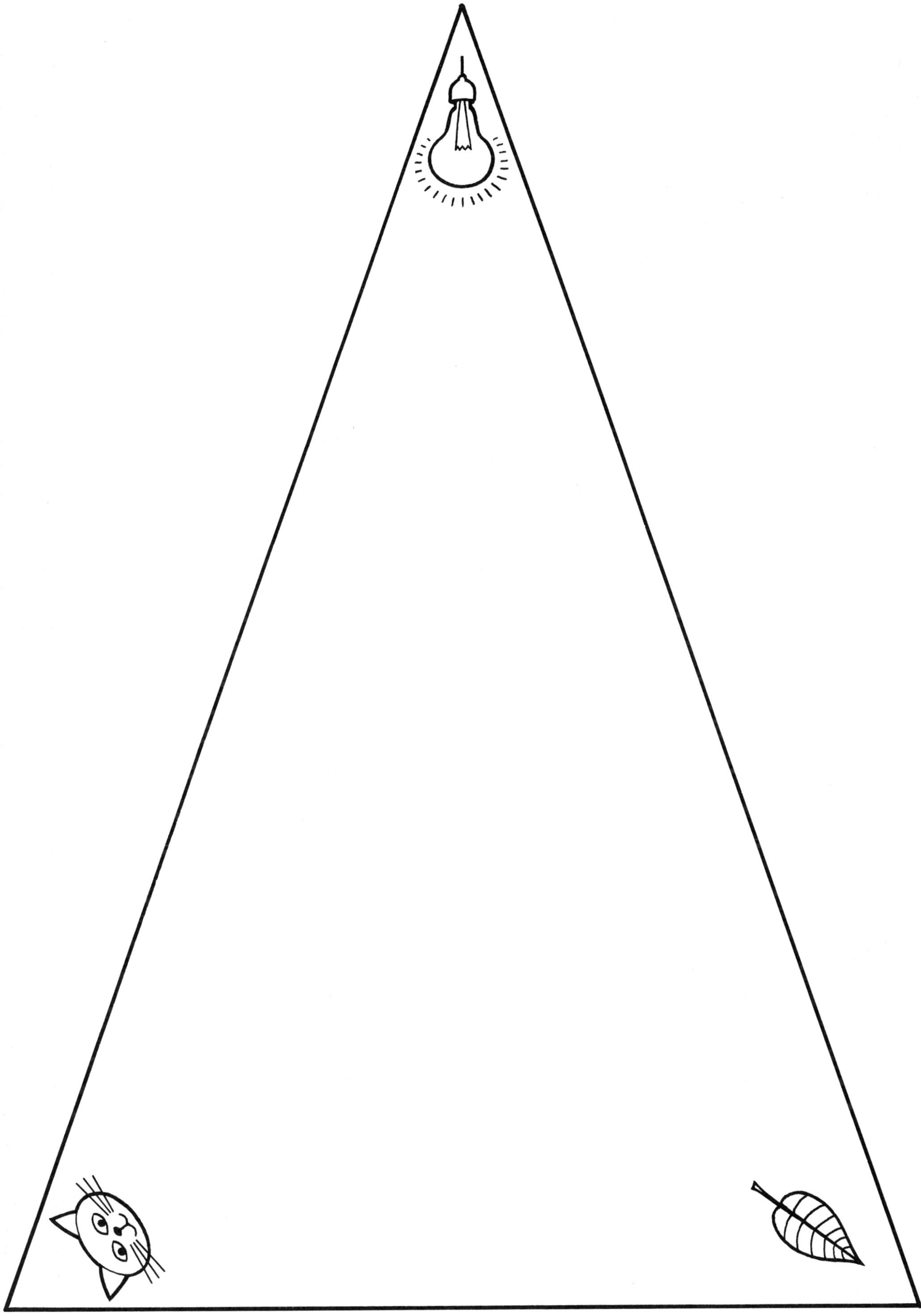

# Folding triangles

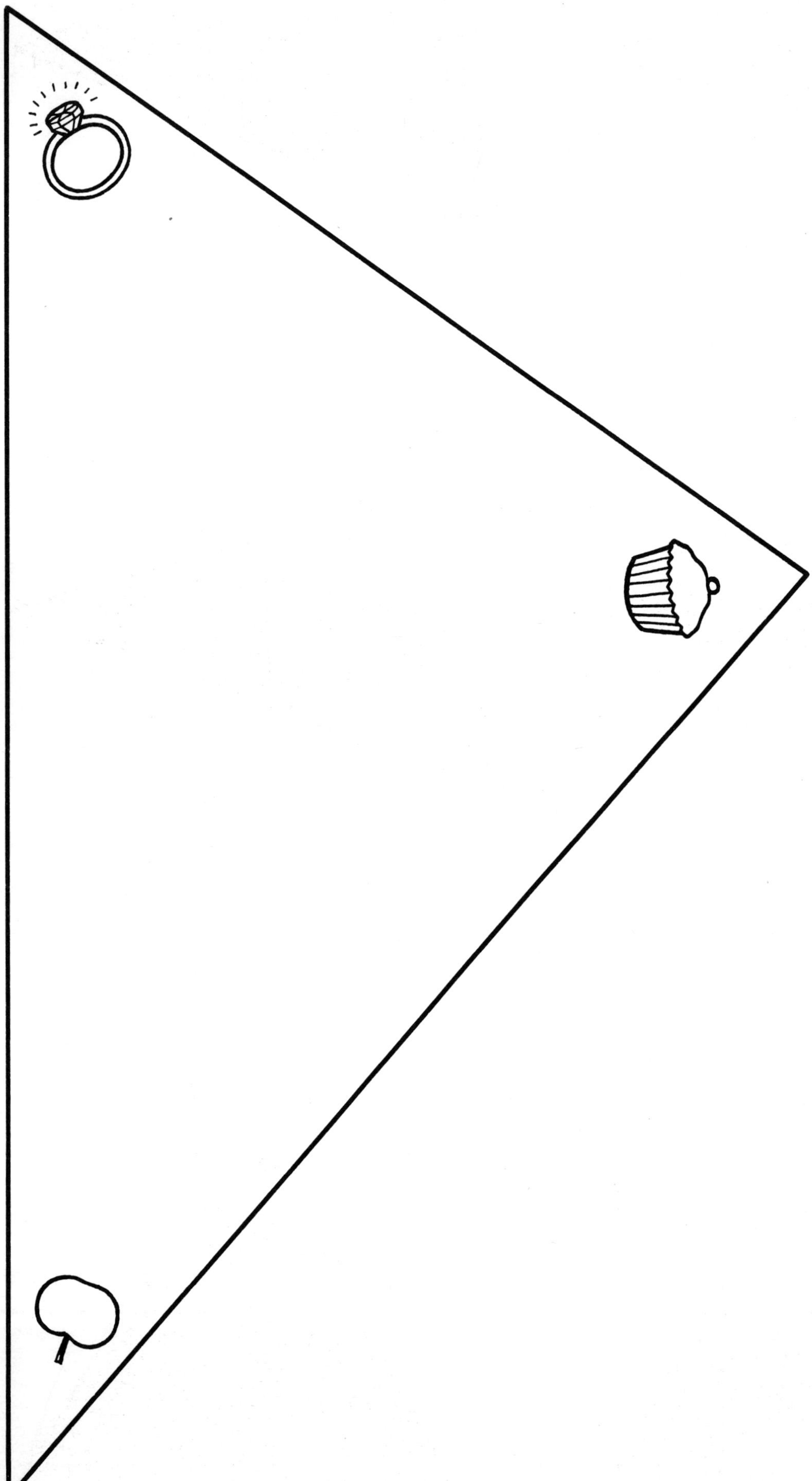

# Fitting triangles

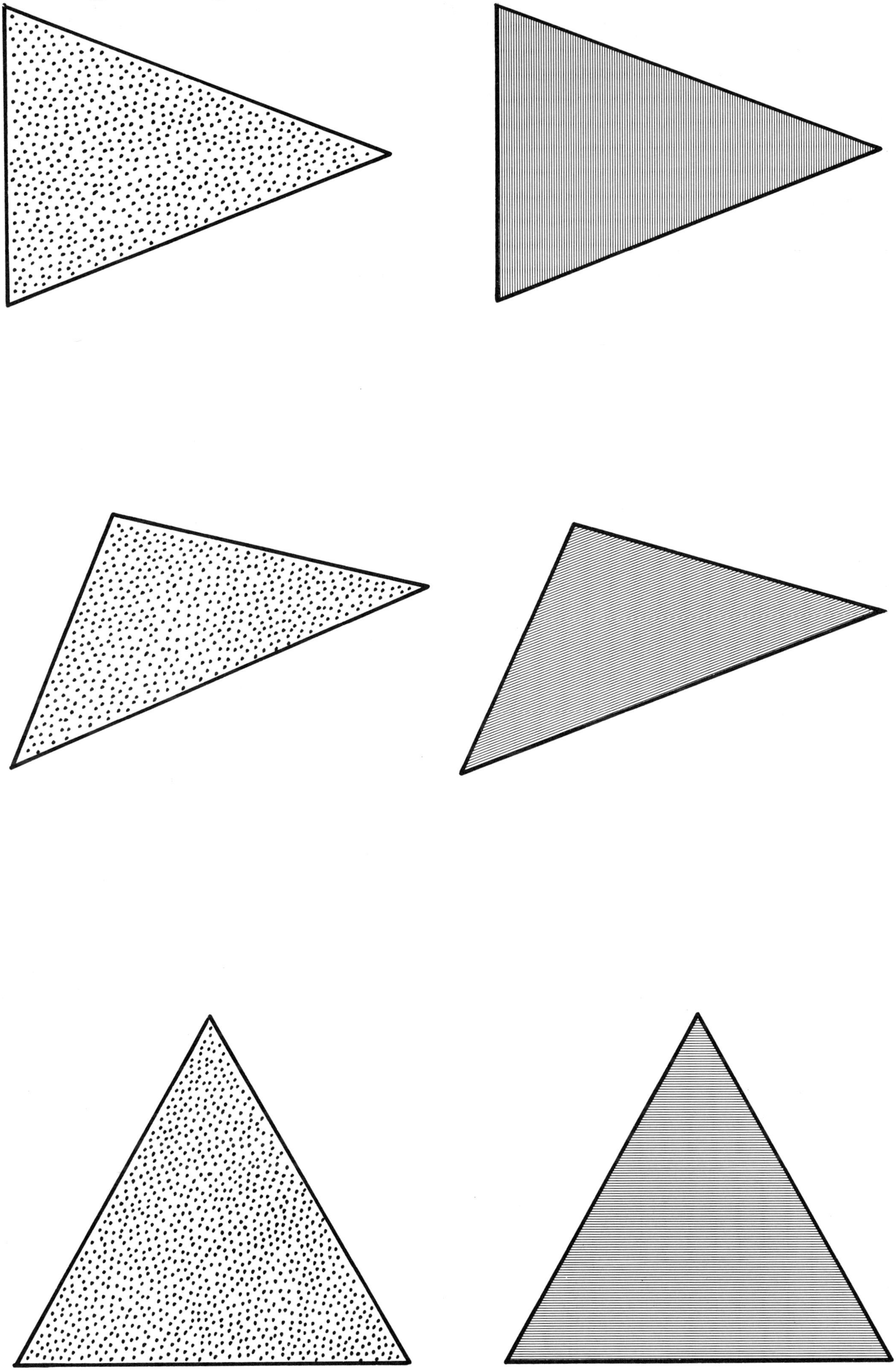

# Fitting triangles

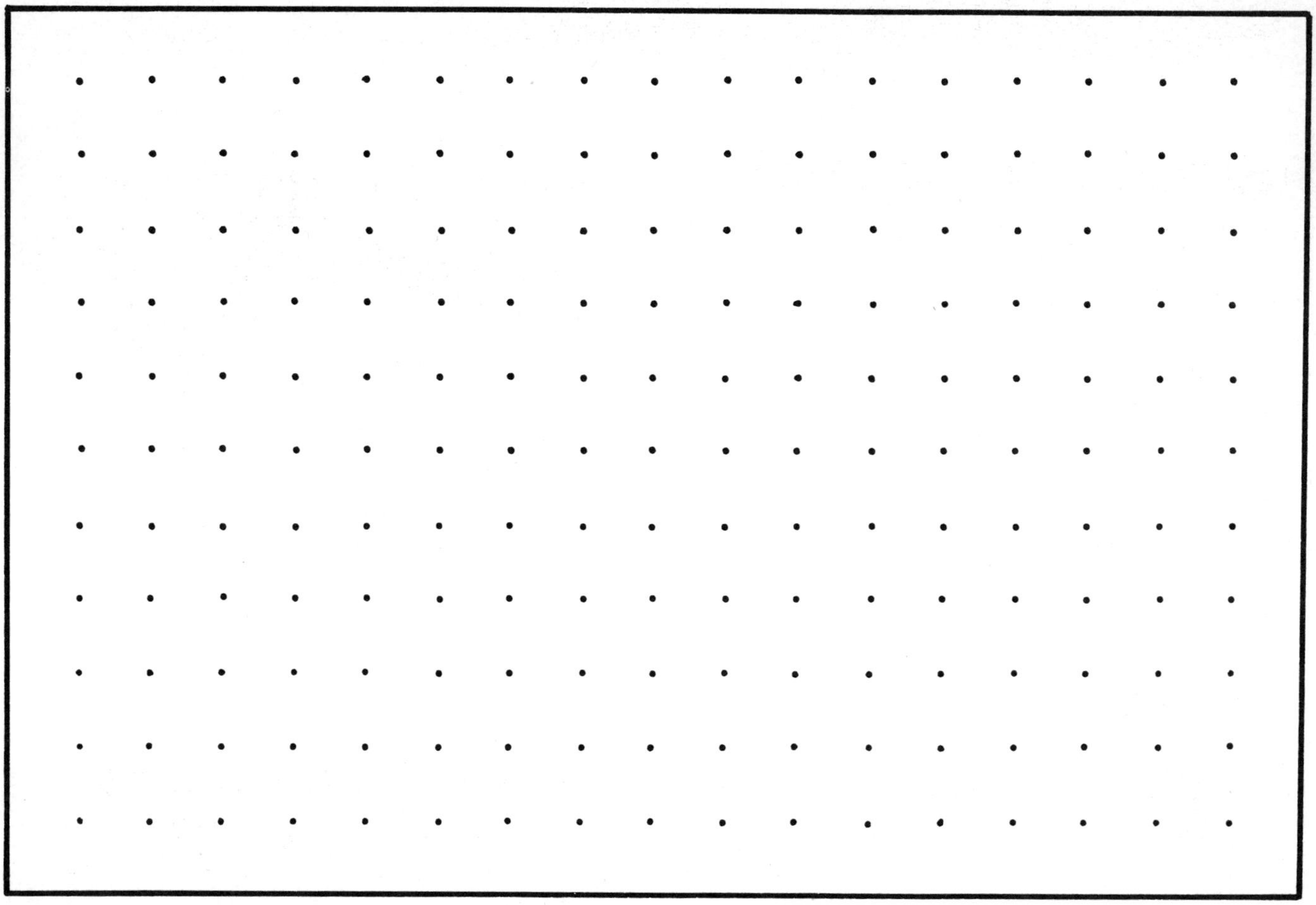

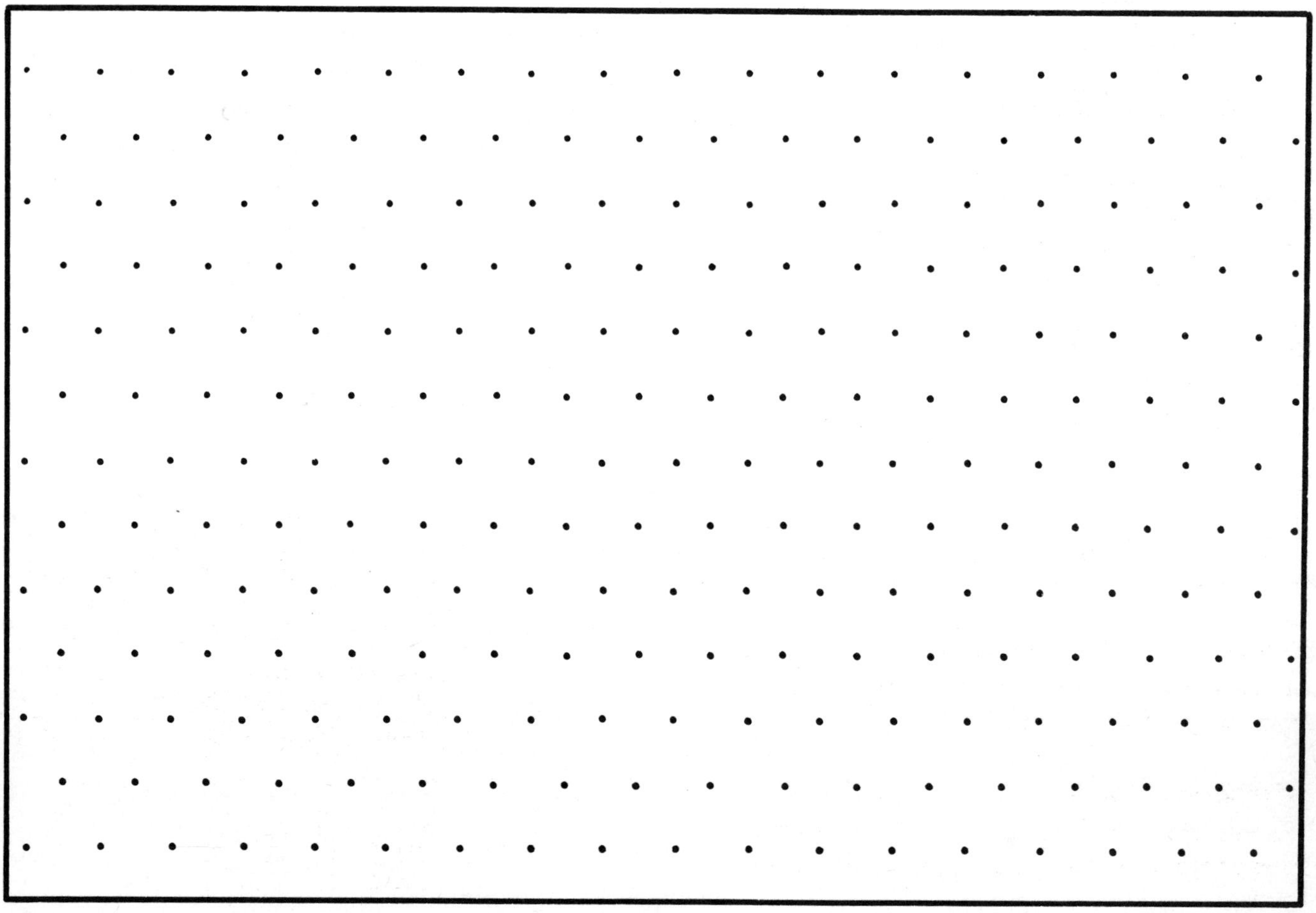

# Quadrilaterals

## Squares from squares

See photocopiable pages 19 and 20.

### Objectives

To continue an alternating spatial pattern. To establish that the four triangles formed by joining the mid-points of the sides of a square can be re-formed into another square, that is half the area of the original.

### Classroom development

Take photocopiable page 19 and look at the pattern.

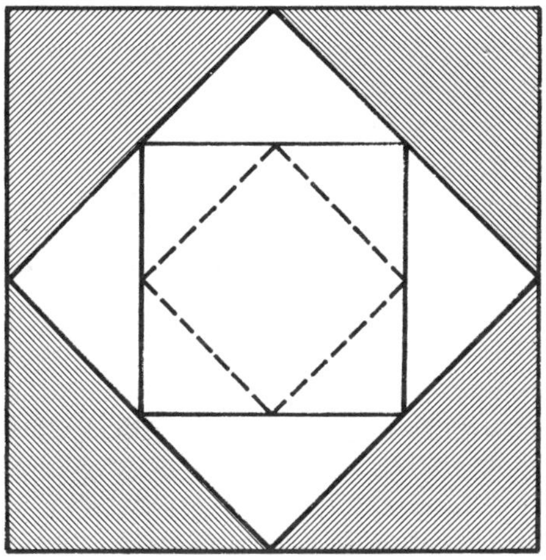

Predict how the next square in the pattern will fit in. Cut out the small square on the sheet and stick it in the correct position. Fold over the shaded triangles, notice how they fit together. Cut off the folded triangles and re-form them into a square. Stick this square on to another piece of paper.

Now cut off the next four triangles and repeat as above. Continue until complete. Discuss the various squares made. What can be said about their sizes?

The relative areas of squares such as these can be further explored by using photocopiable page 20. The square pattern has been started on a squared grid. Complete and extend the design. The steps taken for page 19 can then be carried out.

### Further activities

If 12 sets of squares are cut out, they can be formed into interesting patterns like the one shown.

Alternatively the squares could be made from wallpaper, fabric or used greetings cards.

## Crosses and squares

See photocopiable pages 21 and 22.

### Objectives

To investigate how squares fit together and how quarters of squares relate to each other.

### Classroom development

On photocopiable page 21 colour the cross on each square using only one colour. Cut out the four squares and stick them on to a piece of paper to form a larger square.

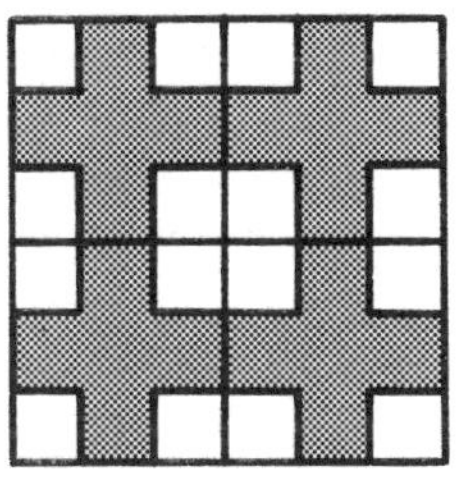

Take photocopiable page 22. Look at one of the large squares. Colour the small squares around the cross and then cut out the large square. Cut along the dotted lines to make four small squares.

Fit these together so that a coloured square is formed in the centre.

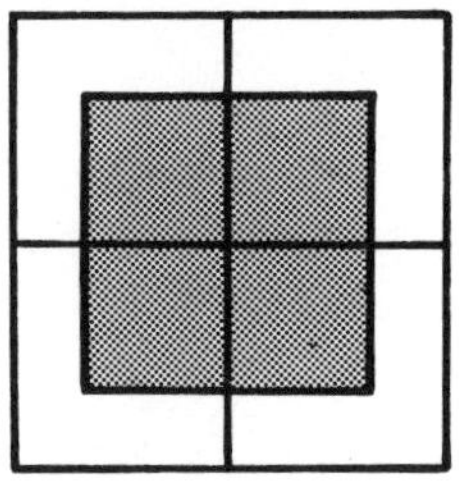

Repeat with the other three large squares. Join all four squares together to make a pattern.

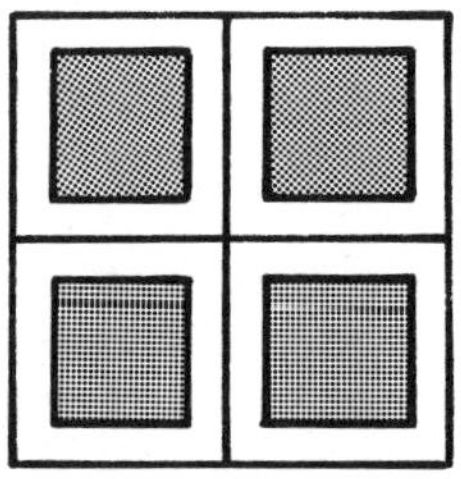

### Further activities

Make other patterns using four quarters of a square. How does each pattern look when repeated? Choose your favourite pattern and stick it on to a large sheet of paper.

## Four equal sides

See photocopiable pages 23 and 24.

### Objectives

To introduce the rhombus, and to investigate its properties.

### Classroom development

Join each group of four dots with straight lines to make four-sided shapes. Tell the children to join the '4' dot to the '1' dot so that they have drawn four lines.

Measure the lengths of the sides of each shape using string or a ruler. Sort the set of shapes which are squares. This can be done by fitting one shape on to another to check for right angles. Each remaining shape is a rhombus.

Investigate folding and turning each rhombus.

### Further activities

Try other combinations of shapes such as rectangles and parallelograms, or squares and rectangles, or rhombuses and parallelograms.

## Three-piece tangram

See photocopiable page 25.

### Objective

To make, recognise and name various polygons from a three-piece tangram.

### Classroom development

Cut out the three tangram pieces. Remake the large square. Discover what shapes can be made with only the two small triangles.

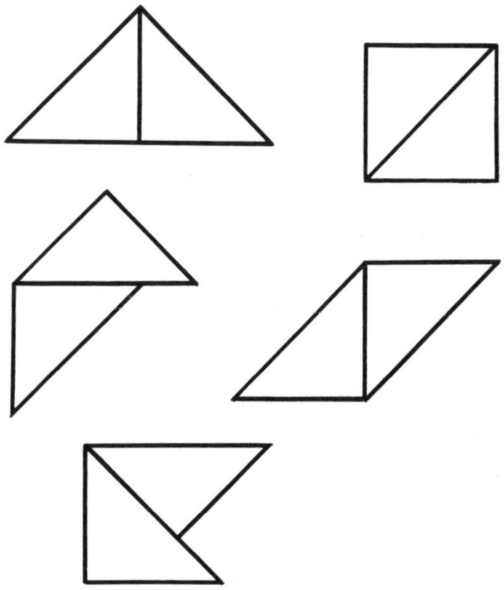

What shapes can be made from all three pieces of the square.

Try to make an isosceles triangle, a parallelogram, a rectangle, an irregular pentagon, an irregular hexagon, and an irregular heptagon.

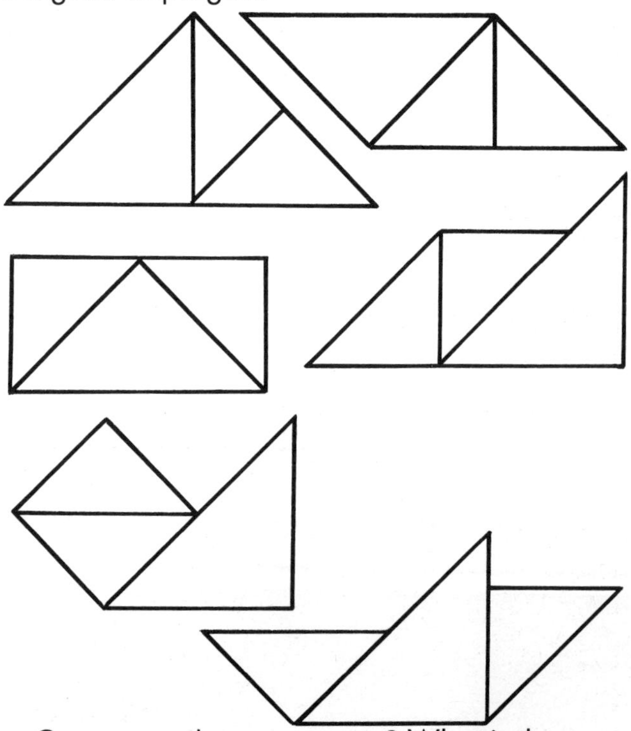

Can you make an octagon? What is the largest number of sides you can make?

# Squares from squares

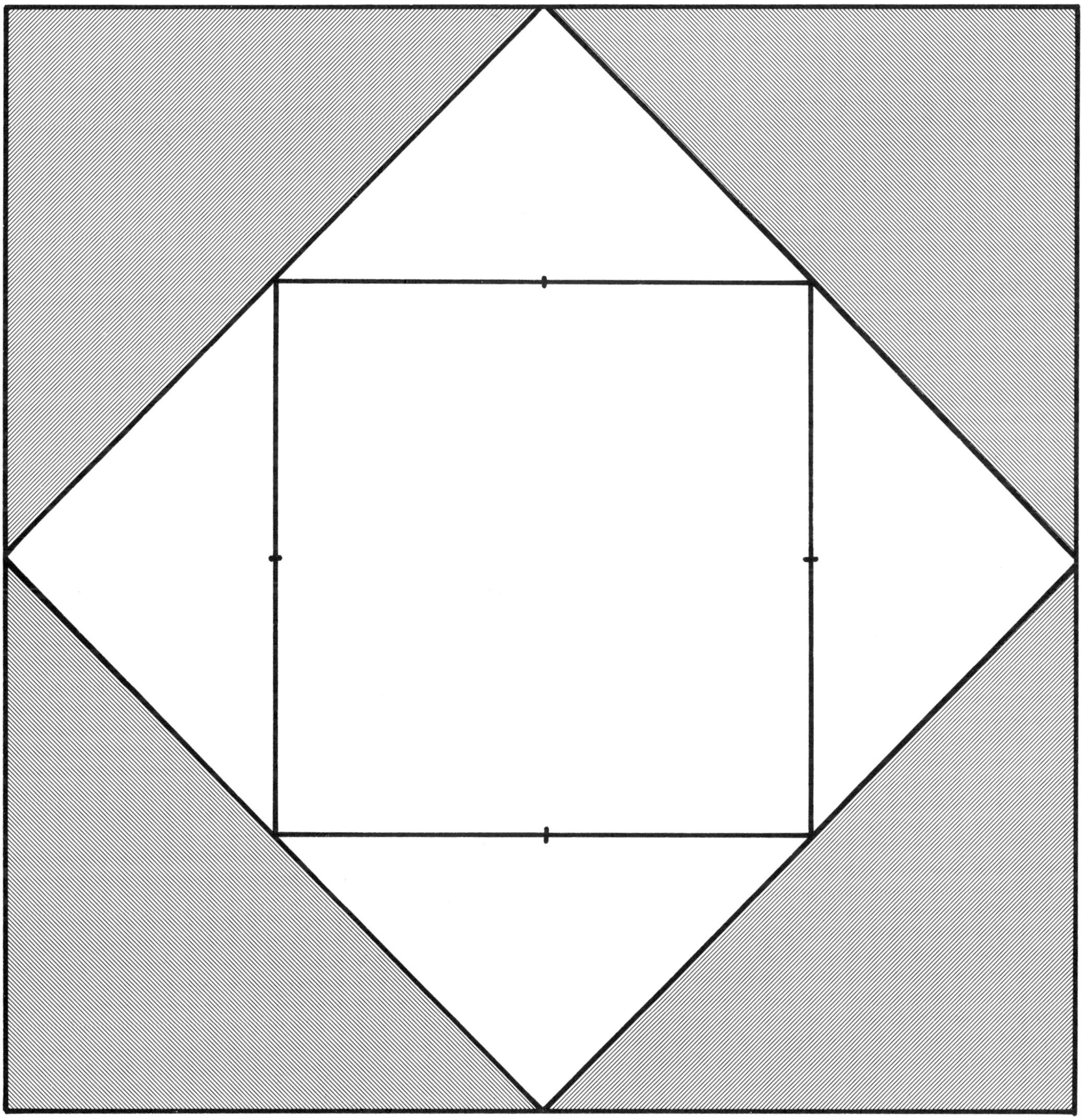

# Squares from squares

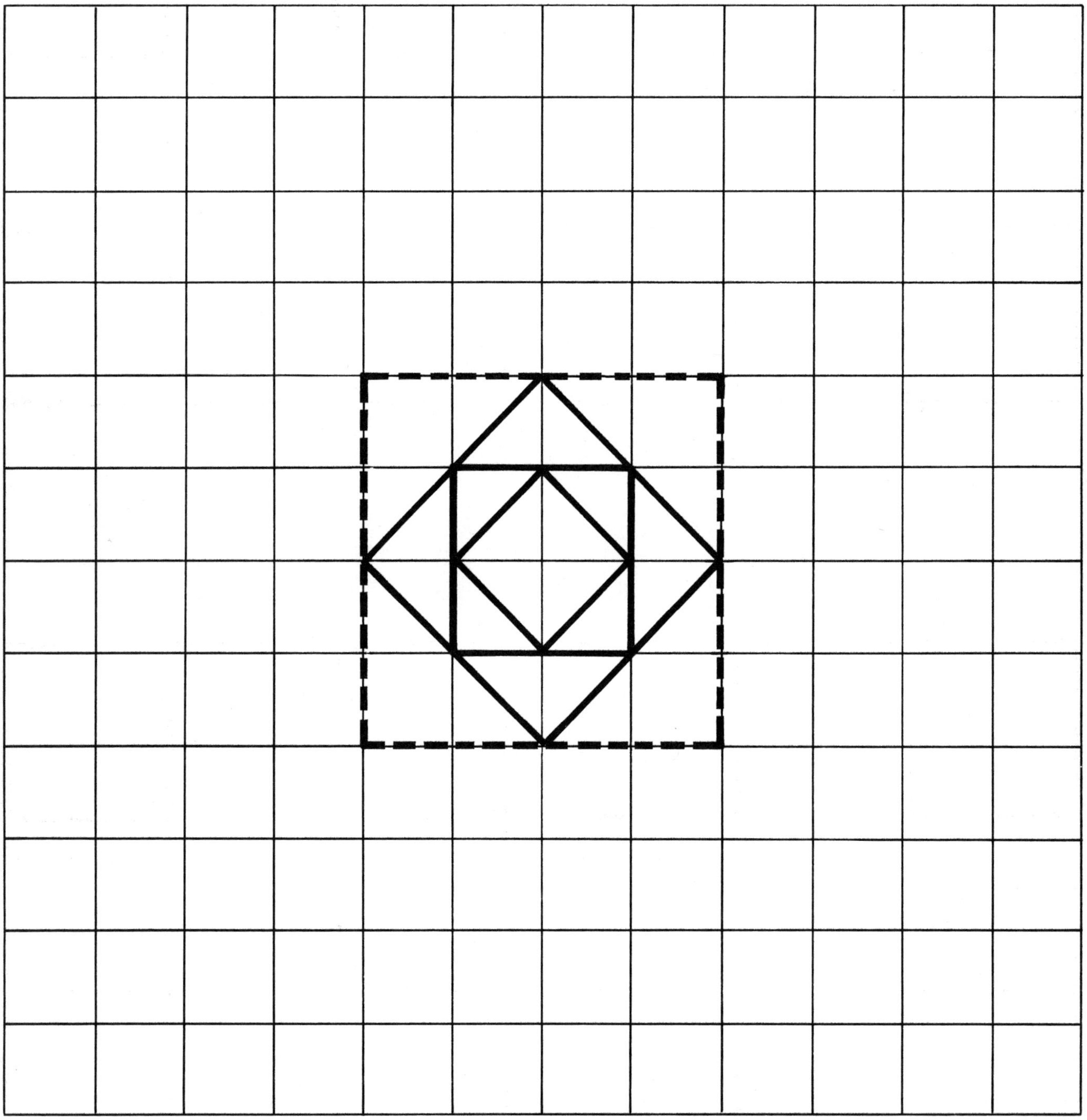

# Crosses and squares

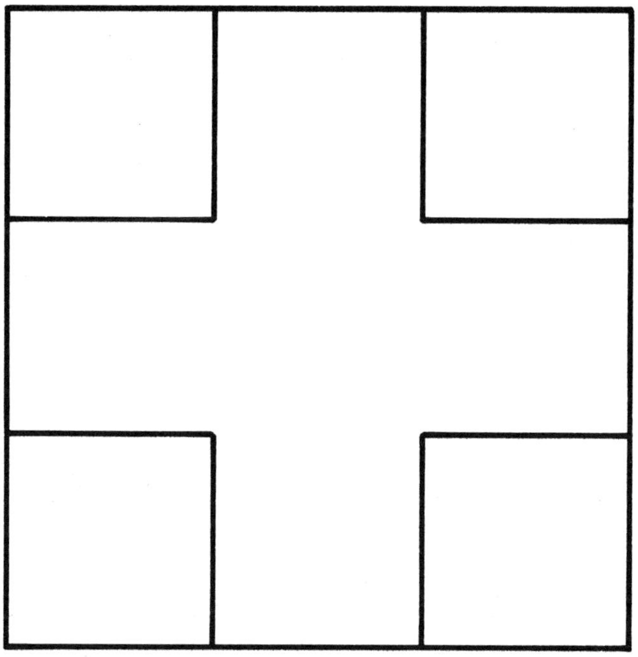

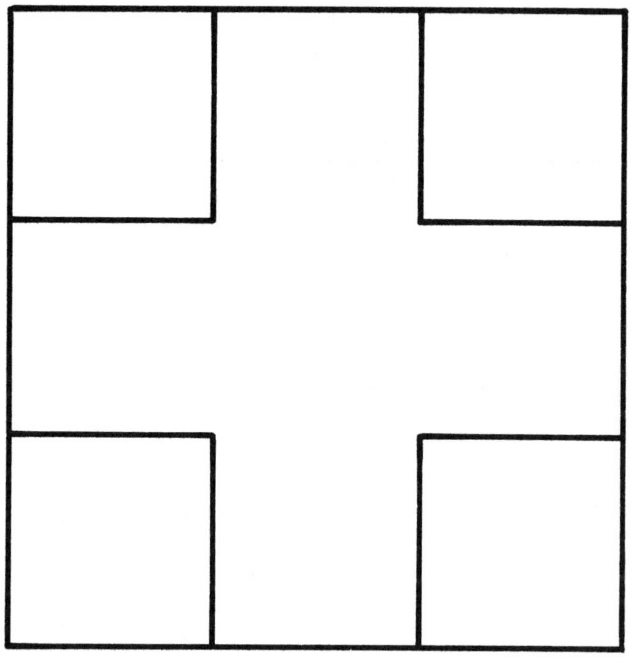

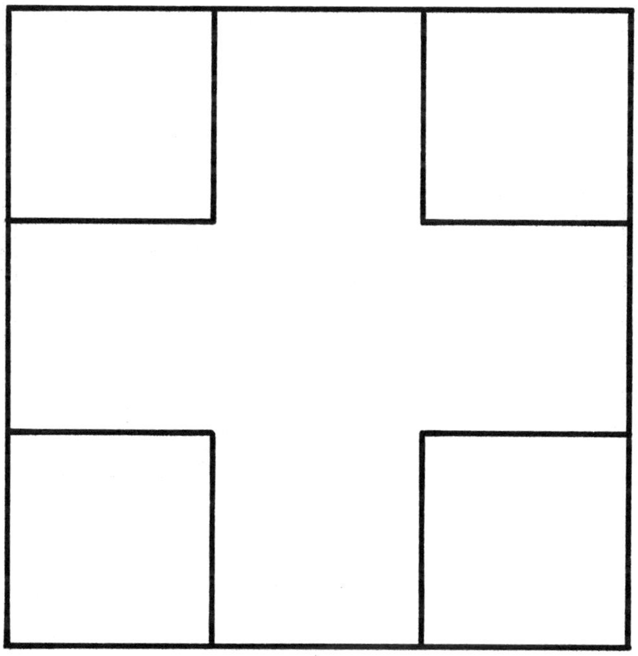

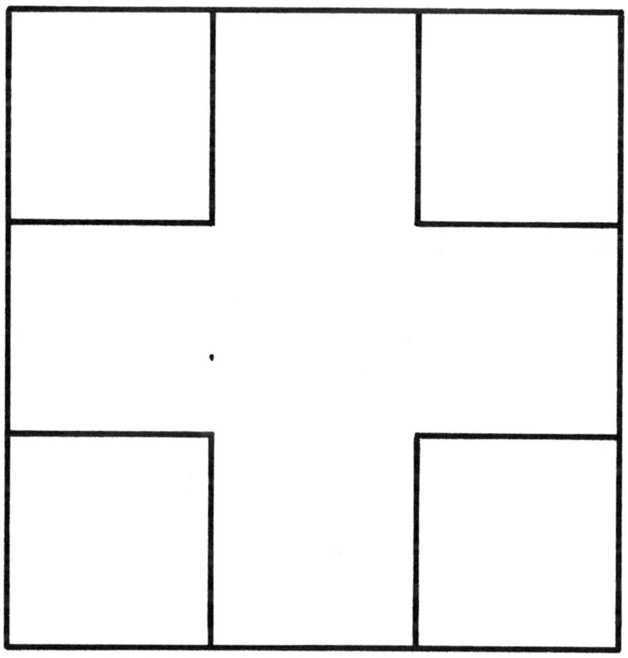

# Crosses and squares

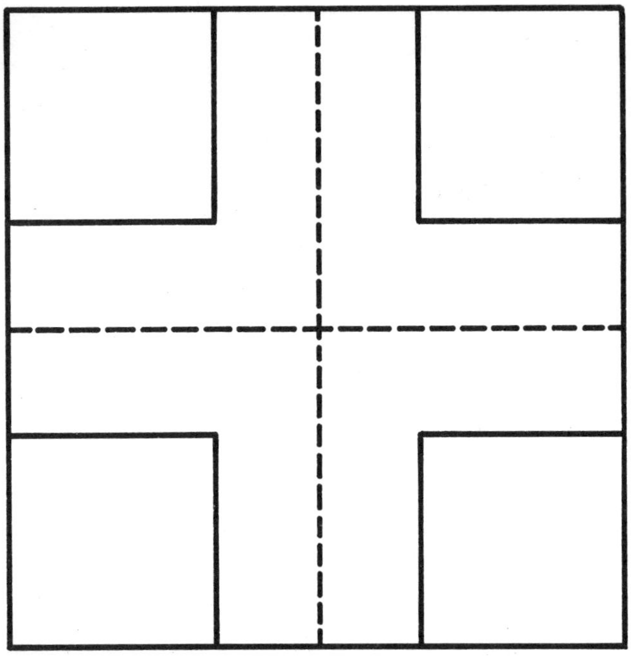

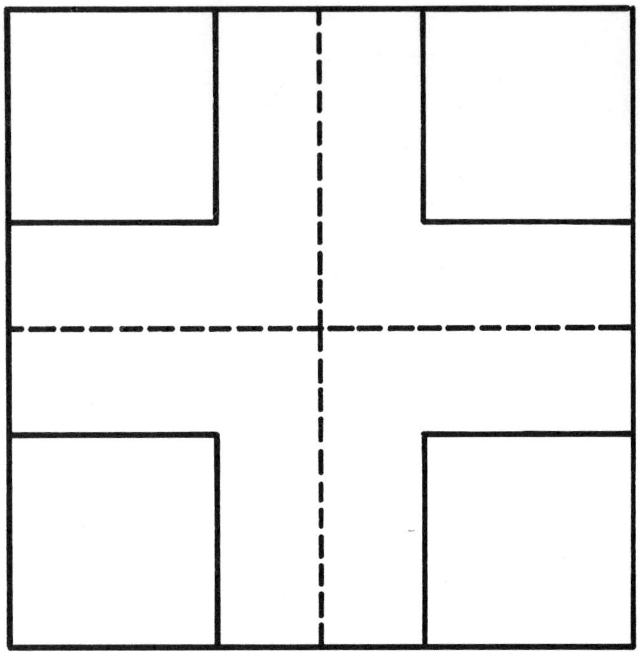

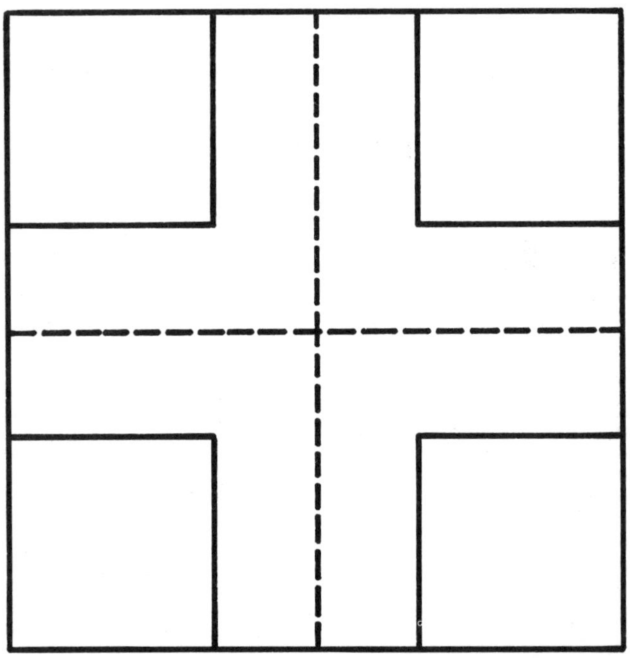

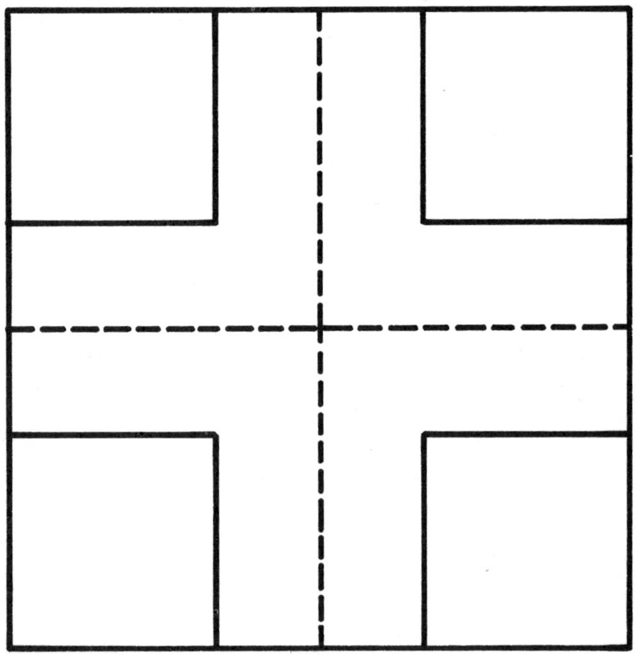

# Four equal sides

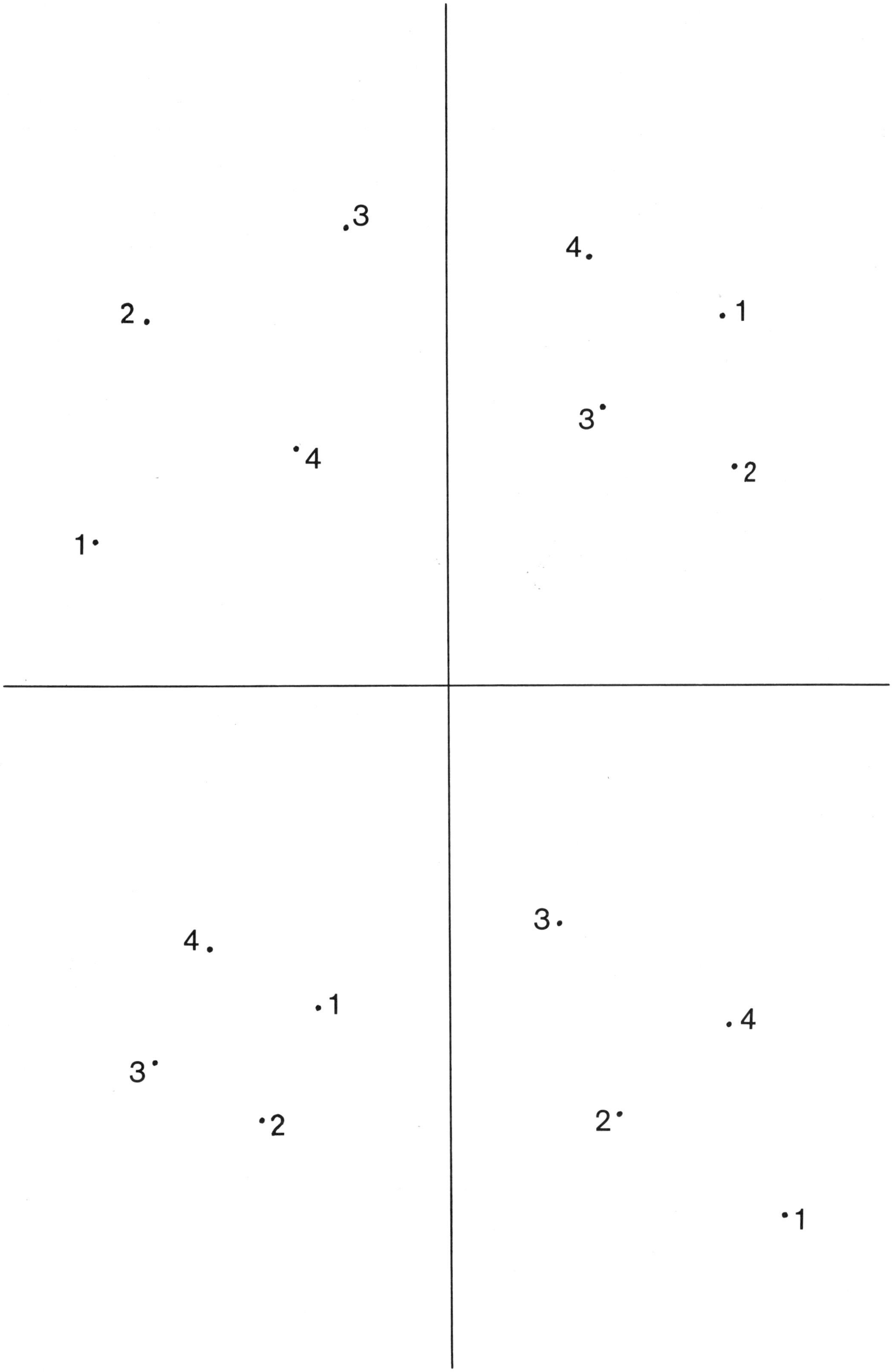

# Four equal sides

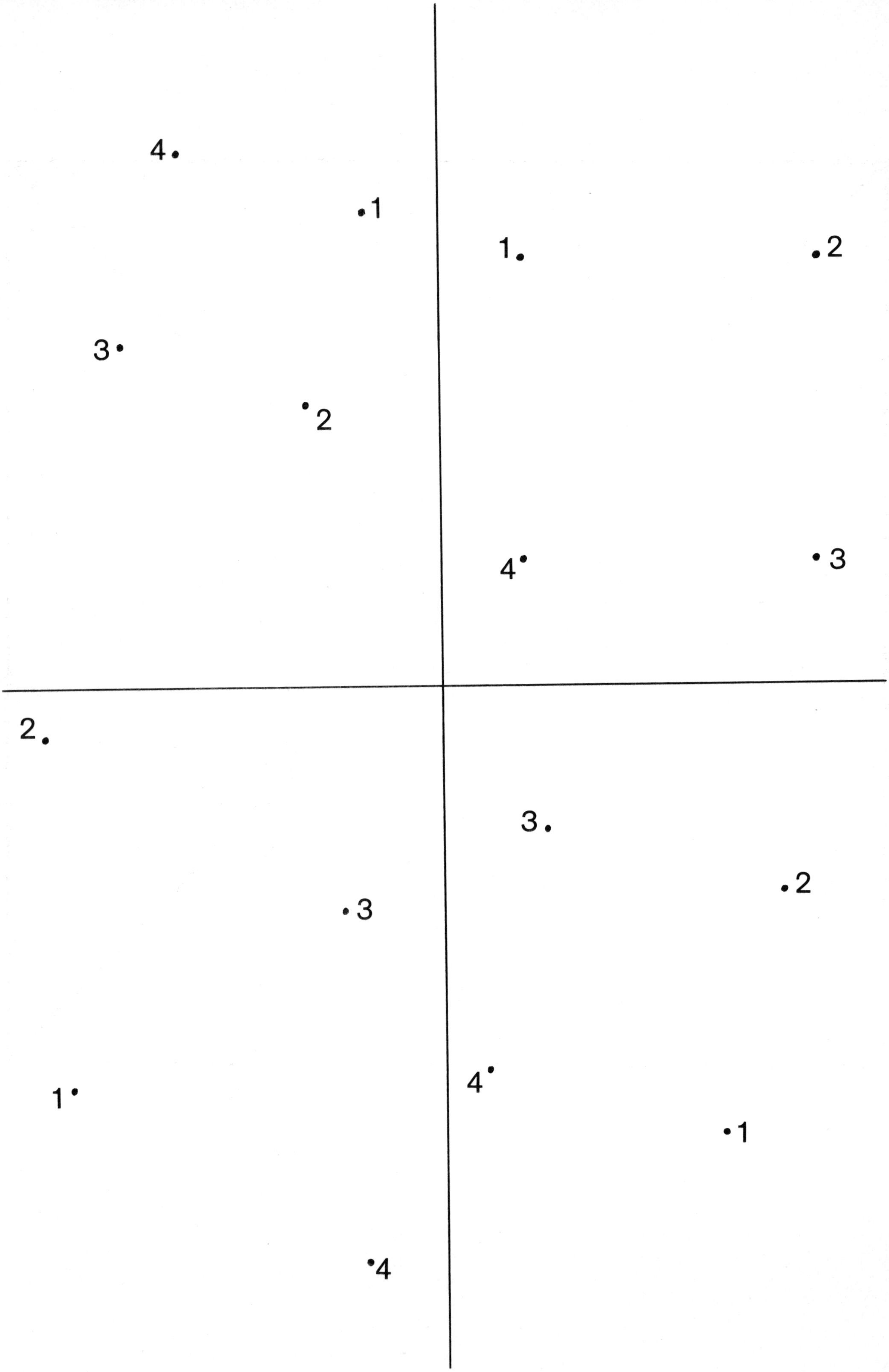

# Three-piece tangram

# Pentagons

## Sorting pentagons

See photocopiable pages 27 and 28.

### Objective

To classify pentagons according to their number of lines of symmetry.

### Classroom development

Cut out the pentagons on pages 27 and 28. Fold each one edge to edge as many times as possible.

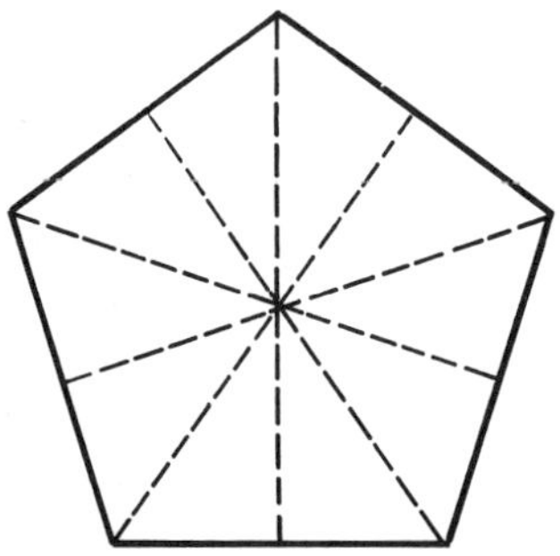

If the two parts match, mark the fold with a coloured line. How many of your pentagons have five coloured folds? How many have one, and how many have no coloured folds? What is the same about the pentagons with the same number of coloured folds? Explore their sides and angles.

## Two-part pentagon

See photocopiable page 29.

### Objectives

To partition a pentagon to create another pentagon and a rhombus. To recognise pentagons with reflex angles.

### Classroom development

Cut out the large marked pentagon on page 29 and cut along the dotted line to make two shapes. Name the shapes. Stick them on to card to use as templates. Tessellate the shapes. What patterns can be made?

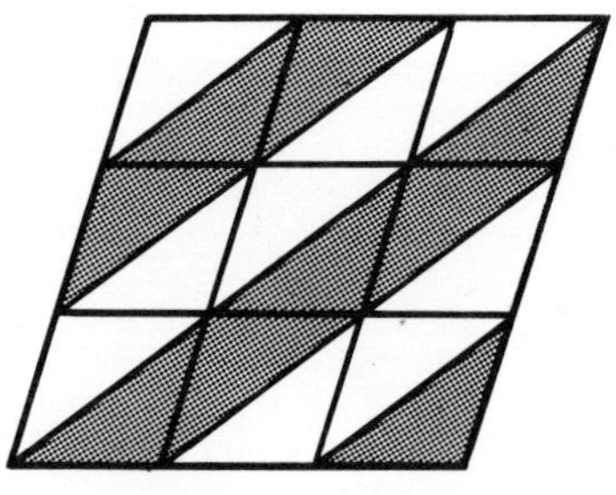

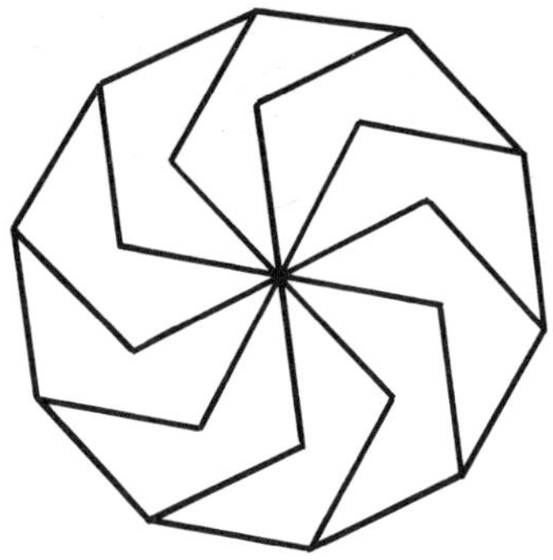

### Further activities

Cut out the plain pentagon. Fold it in half and cut along the fold. Use the pieces as templates to make other patterns.

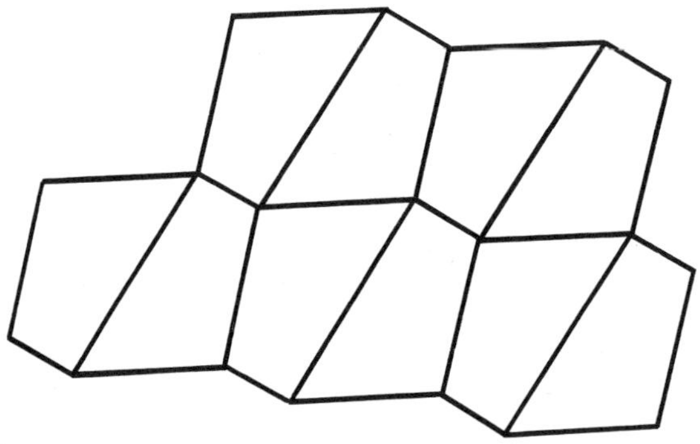

## Stars

See photocopiable page 30.

### Objective

To tessellate and to rotate pentagons.

### Classroom development

Cut out the six pentagons on page 30. Using the completely shaded pentagon as the centre, arrange the others around the centre pentagon to make a star pattern.

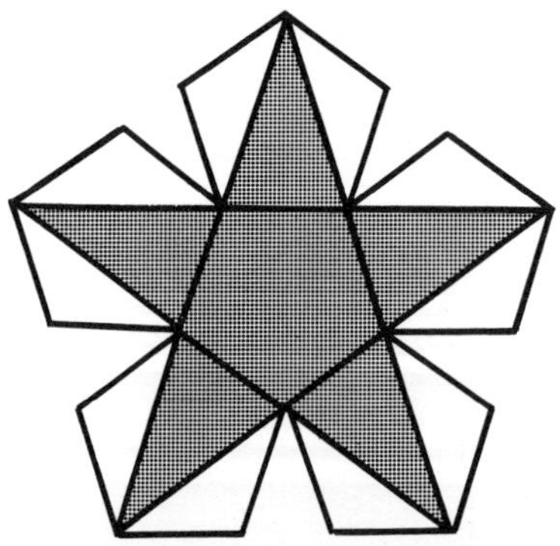

Rotate each of the outer pentagons clockwise. Look at the design now. Rotate the outer pentagons again and look at the design. Rotate again to return to the original star.

# Sorting pentagons

# Sorting pentagons

# Two-part pentagon

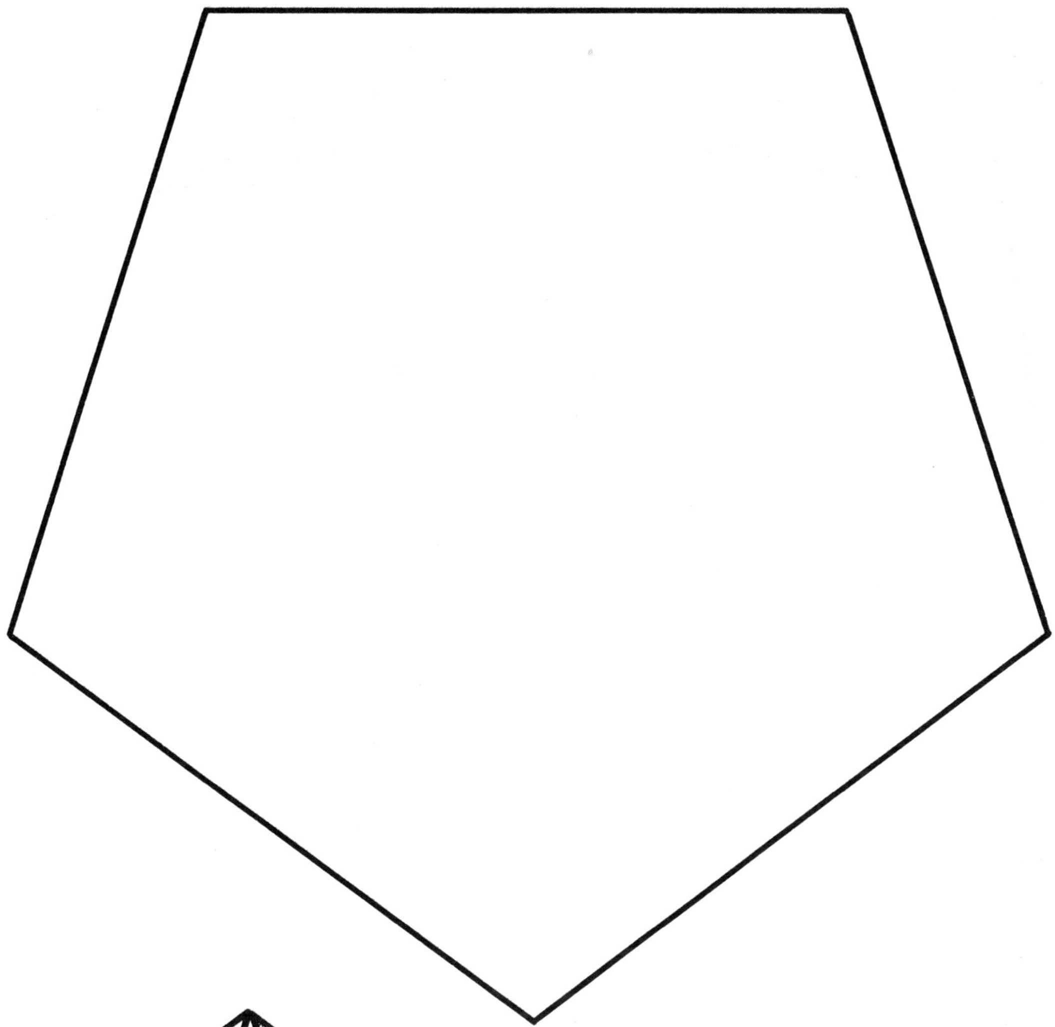

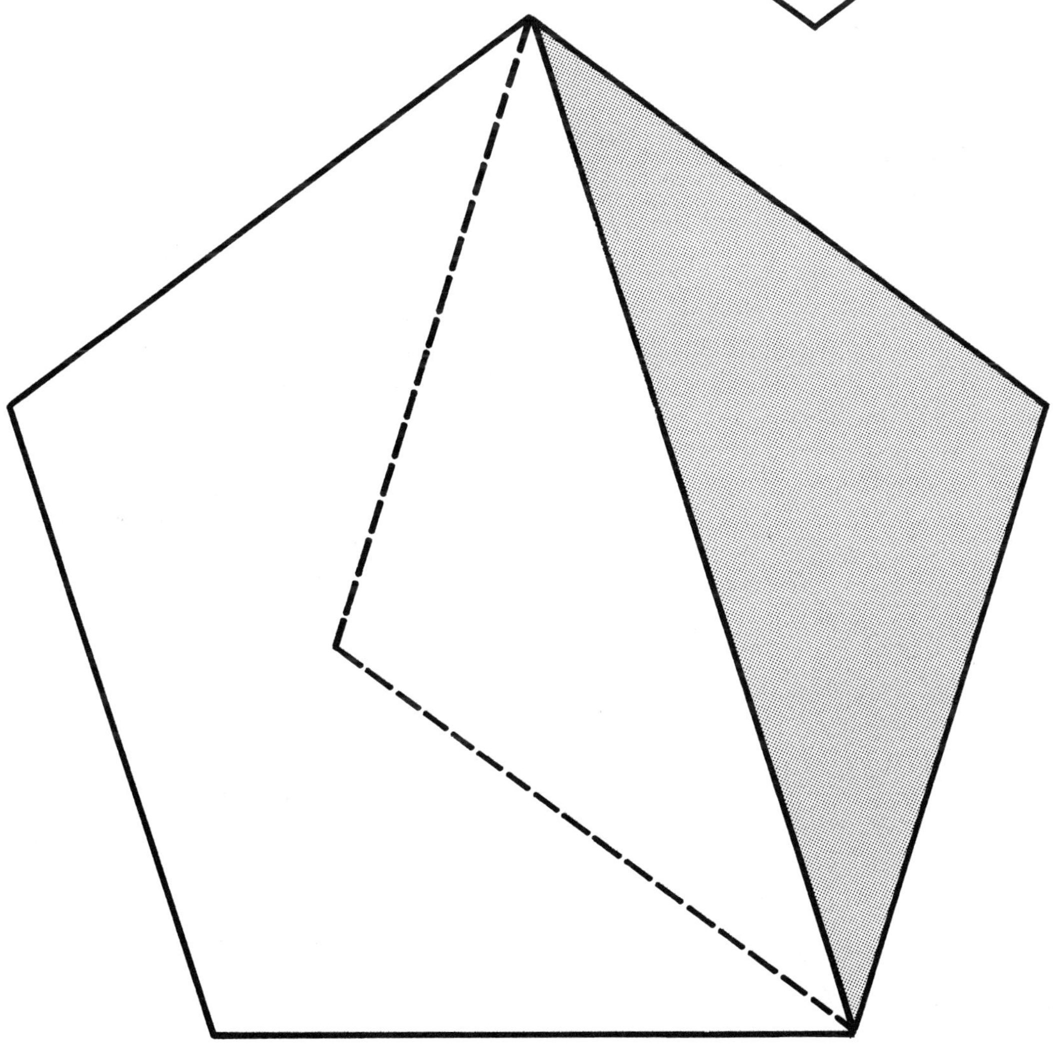

# Stars

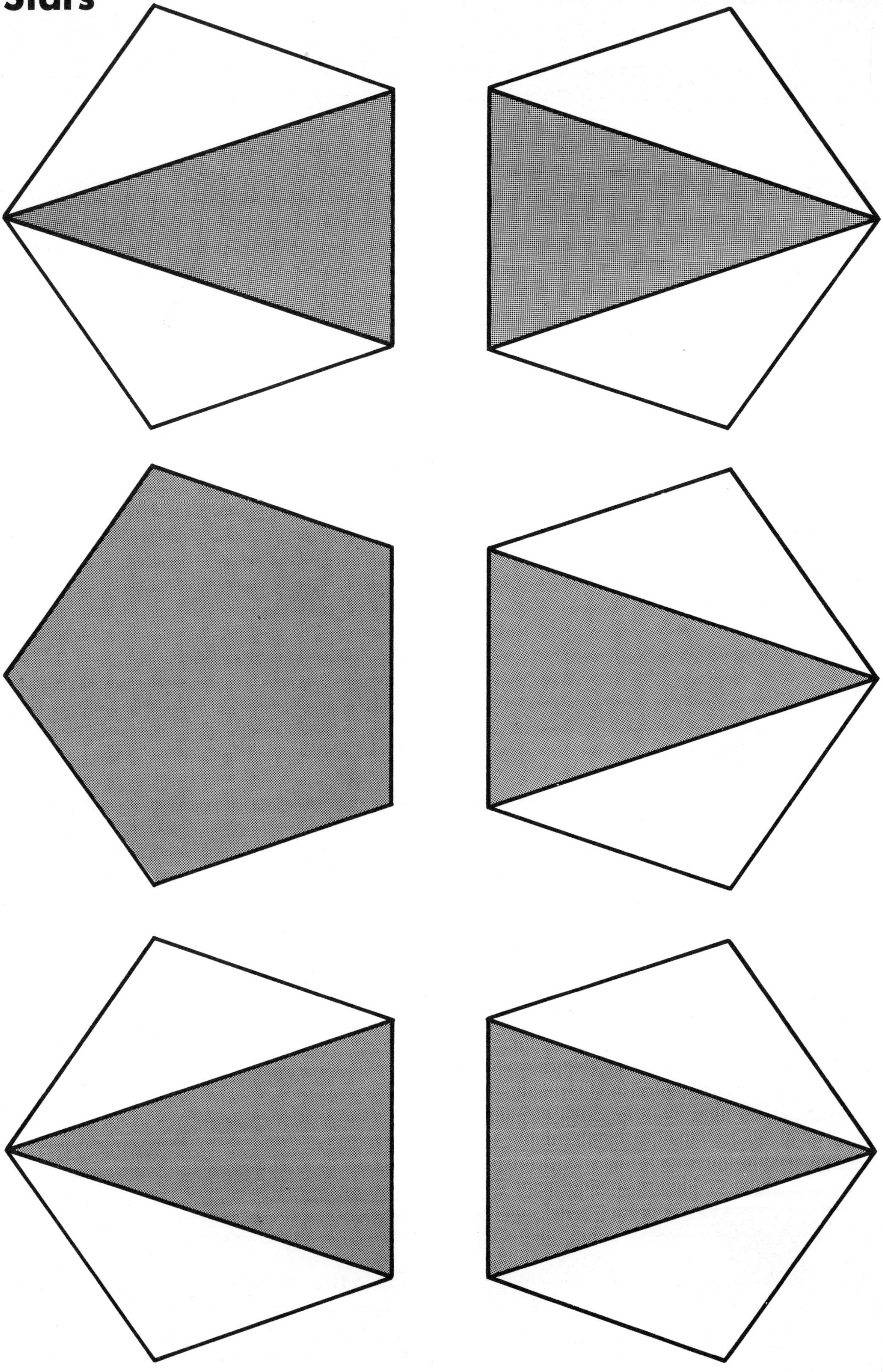

# Hexagons

## Make hexagons

See photocopiable page 33.

### Objective

To fold a hexagon from a circle. To discover that a regular hexagon can be formed from six equilateral triangles.

### Classroom development

Colour the triangle in the circle red (see page 33). Colour the outside sections green. Cut out the circle. Fold back the green outside sections along the lines. Turn the paper over so that the green sections can be seen. Fold the points of the triangle to the centre. What shape have you folded? How many small red triangles can you see? How many small green triangles can you see?

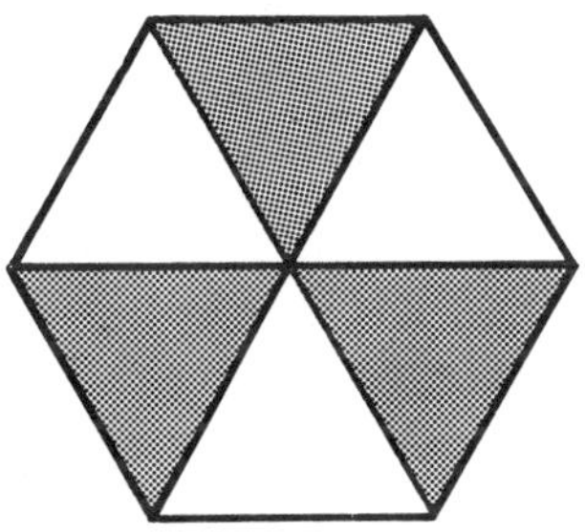

Turn the hexagon over. What do you notice? How can you make this hexagon two-coloured?

Take the six equilateral triangles on page 33. Colour three one colour and the other three another colour. Cut them out and use them to make another two-coloured hexagon. How many different colour arrangements can be made?

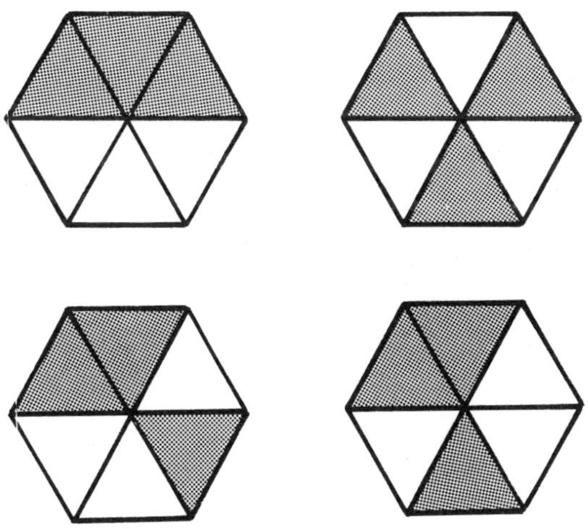

### Further activities

Still using two colours but varying how many triangles you have of each, make as many hexagons as possible. For instance, with four triangles one colour and two triangles another colour these arrangements are possible:

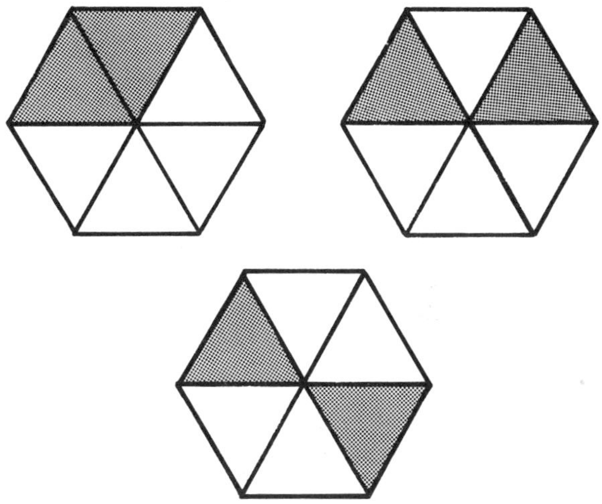

## Tessellating hexagons

See photocopiable page 34.

### Objective

To tessellate regular hexagons.

### Classroom development

You will need two copies of page 34. Colour the sections of the triangles. Make each triangle identical to all the others. One triangle on the page is upside-down and care will need to be taken to ensure six identically coloured triangles.

Cut out the triangles and stick them, in the shape of a hexagon, on to a backing sheet. Use several hexagons to make a large tessellation of hexagons to display. The large hexagons could be outlined in another colour to emphasise their edges.

### Further activities

Investigate, collect and display hexagonal tessellations from a variety of sources such as honeycombs, patchwork and paving slabs.

# Inside the hexagon

See photocopiable pages 35 and 36.

## Objectives

To investigate joining the corners of a hexagon and joining the mid-points of the sides.

## Classroom development

On page 35 join the faces with straight lines. What shape have you drawn?

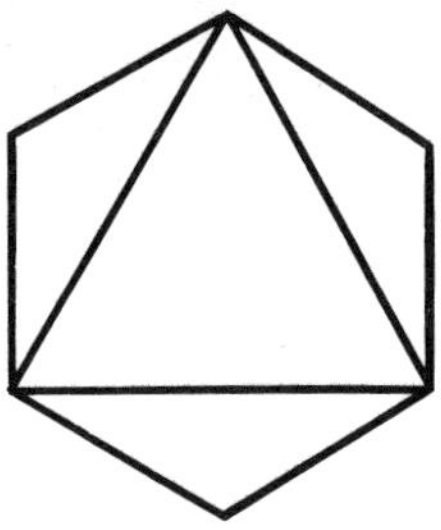

Now join the suns together in the same way. What shapes can you see? How many isosceles triangles are there? How many equilateral triangles are there?

Join the suns and the faces on page 36. Investigate the shapes drawn. How many equilateral triangles are there? How many rhombuses are there?

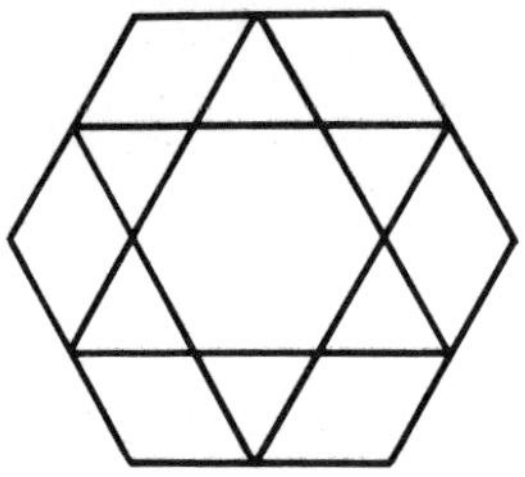

## Further activities

Using page 36 join the adjacent suns and faces. What shape have you drawn?

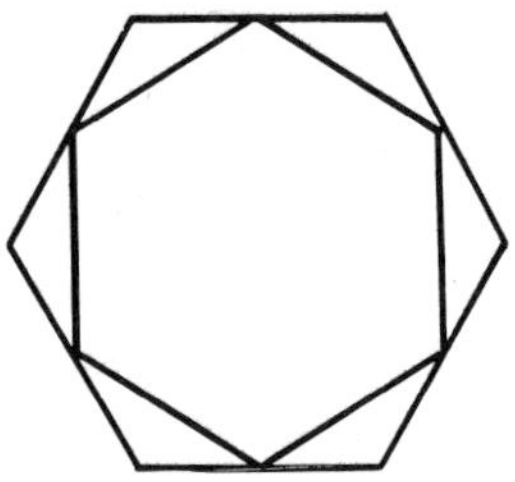

Find the mid-point of each of the lines drawn and join them up. What has happened? Can you continue?

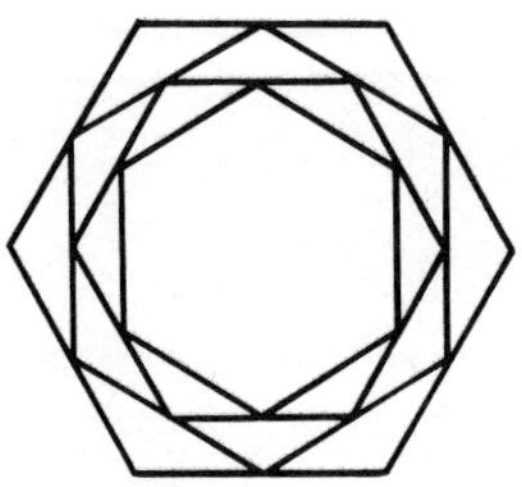

# Chevrons

See photocopiable pages 37 and 38.

## Objectives

To recognise irregular hexagons and to tessellate them.

## Classroom development

Colour the hexagons on page 37 identically. Then tessellate them. For example:

Explore a variety of arrangements and try to form a regular hexagon.

Notice the central hexagon. Try out your own designs on the hexagons on page 38.

# How many colours?

See photocopiable page 39.

## Objectives

To form a pattern, make a hypothesis and to predict what happens next.

## Classroom development

Cut out the large group of hexagons. Use the least number of colours possible to colour the hexagons so that no hexagon touches another hexagon of the same colour. It may be helpful to use different coloured plastic counters and only colour the hexagons where you are sure. Look at the patterns of colour. What do you notice?

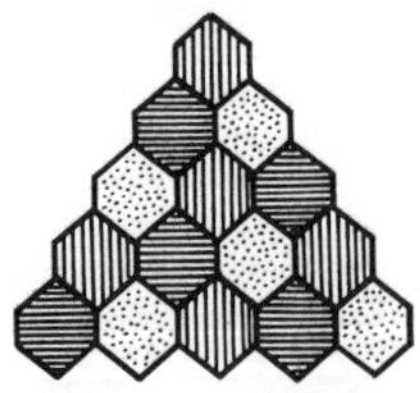

Predict the sequence of colours in the next row of hexagons. Cut out the strip of hexagons and test your theory. What would happen if the group of hexagons continued to grow?

## Further activities

Use wallpaper or fabric to make three-colour designs.

# Make hexagons

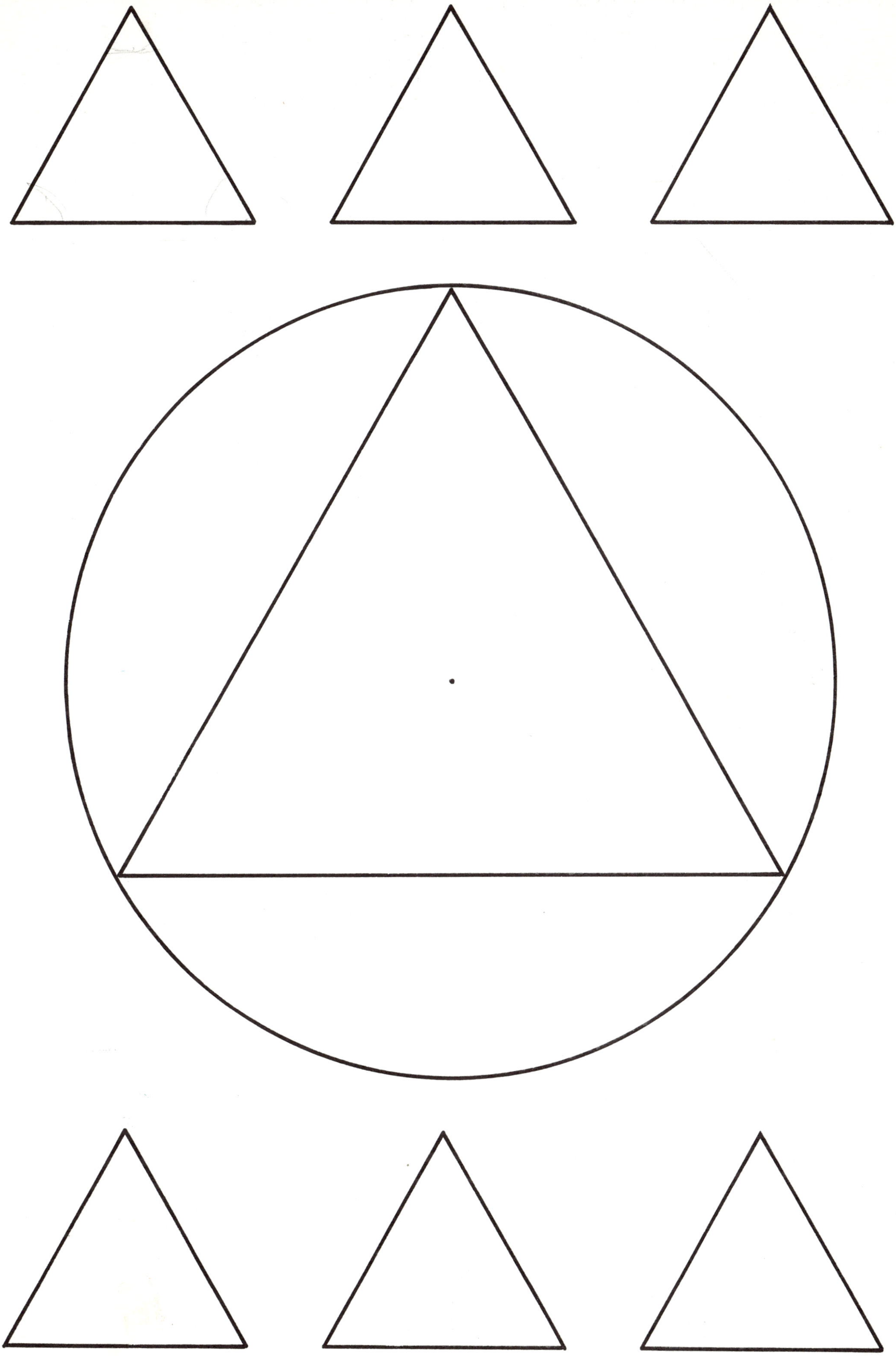

# Tessellating hexagons

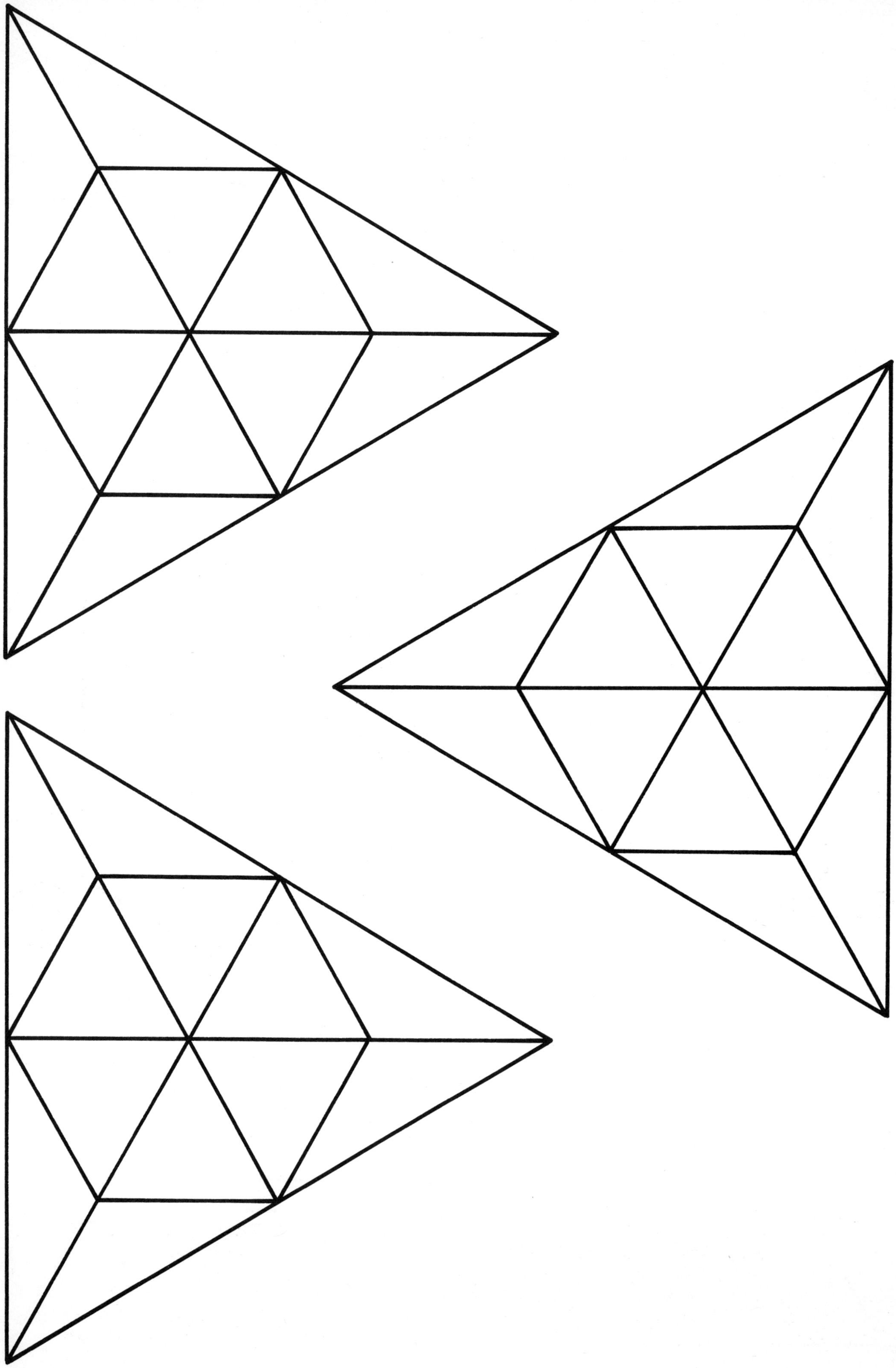

# Inside the hexagon

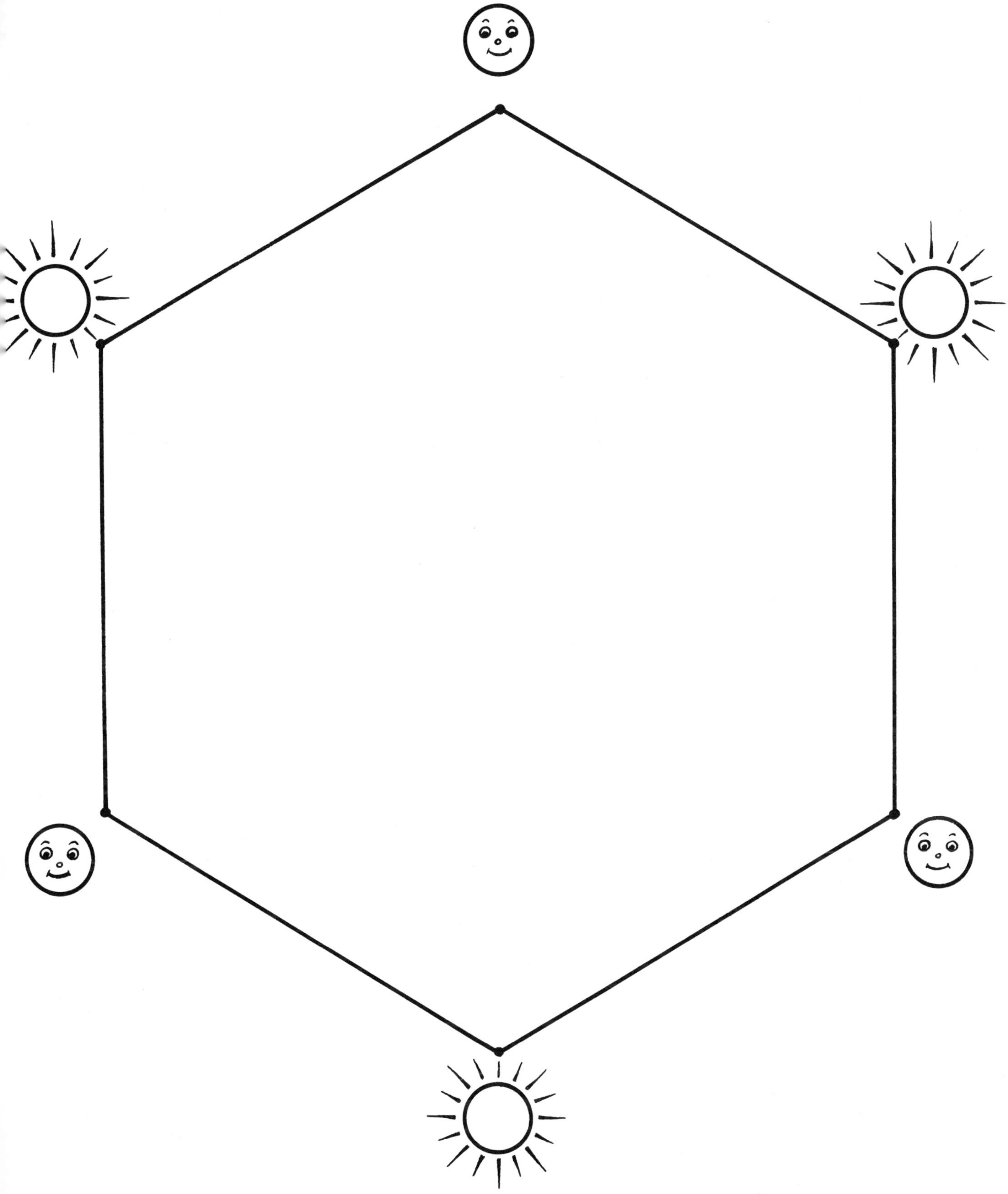

# Inside the hexagon

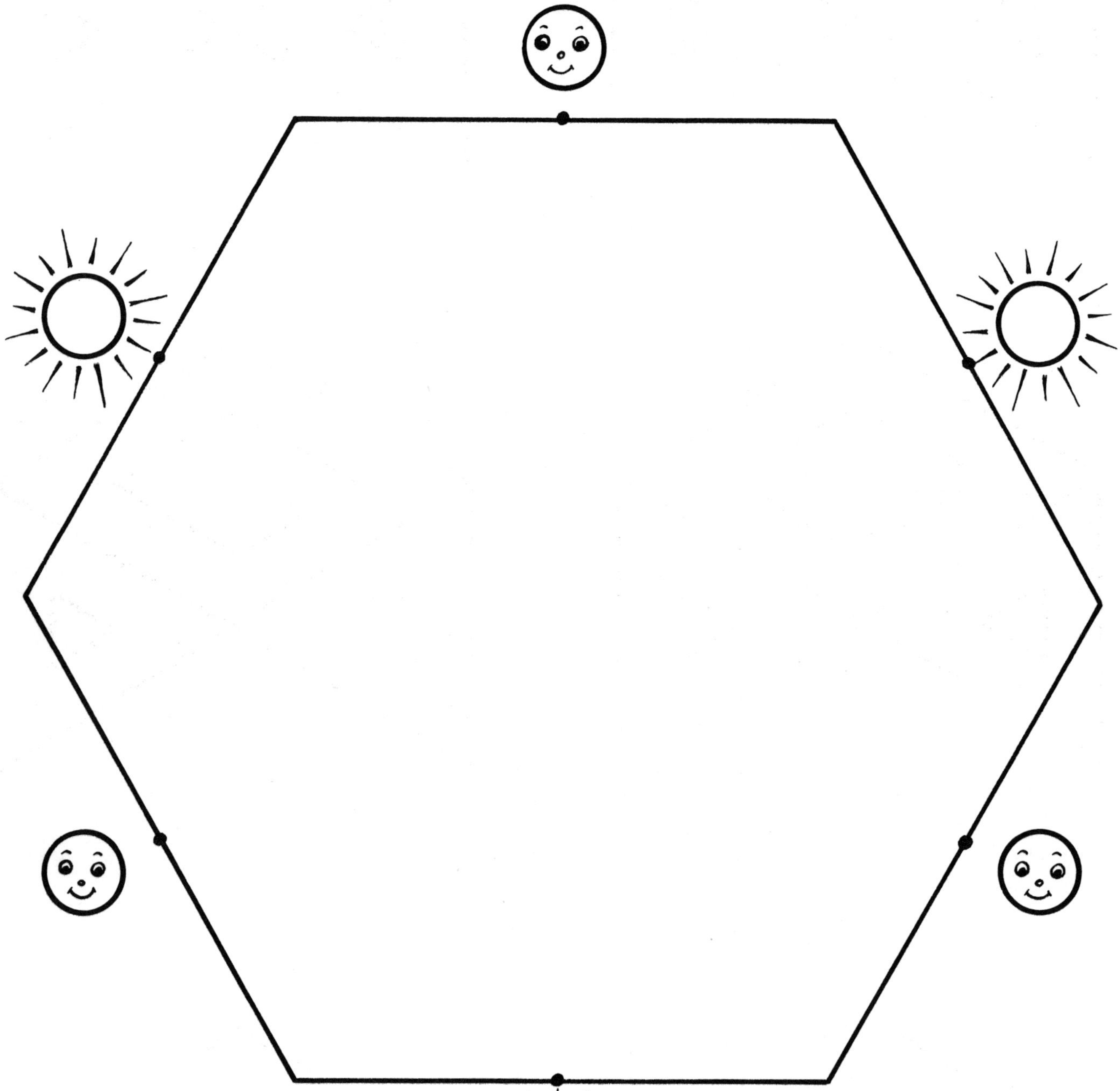

## Chevrons

# Chevrons

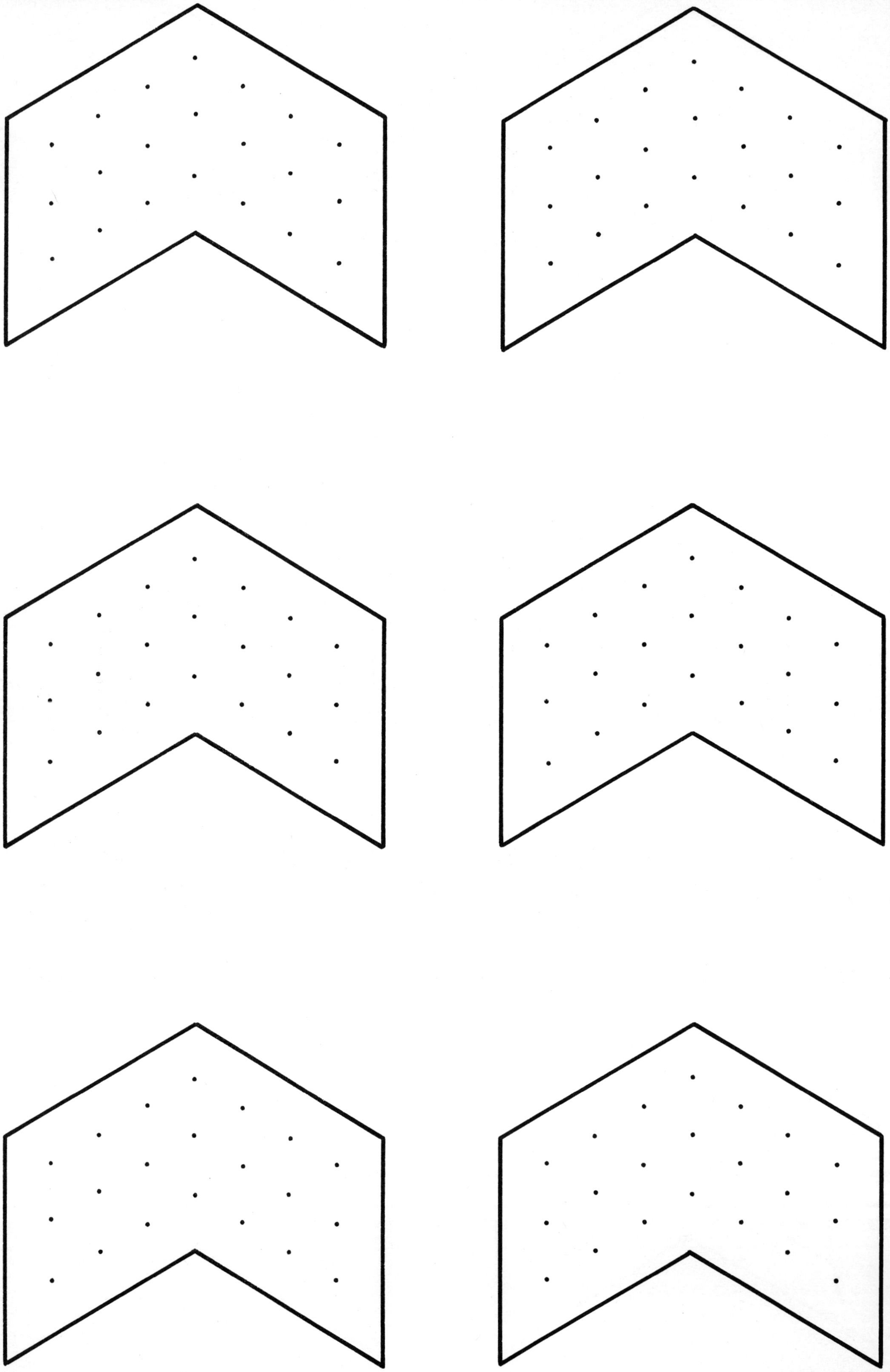

# How many colours?

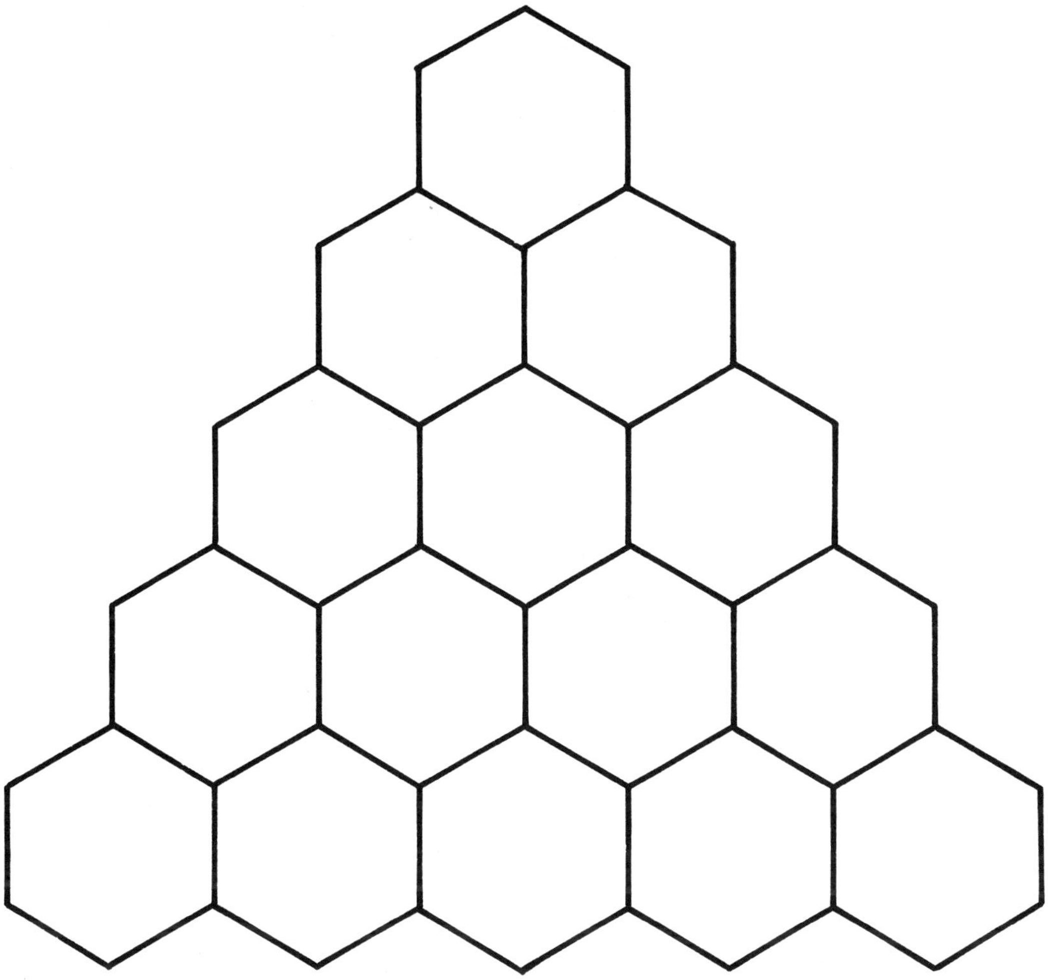

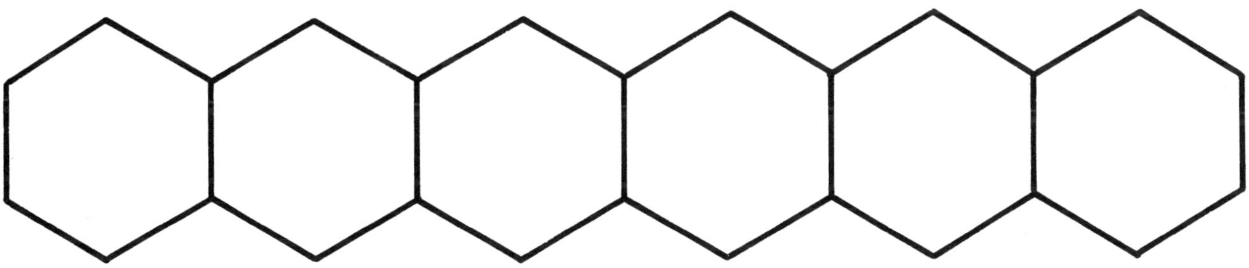

# Circles

## Square on the circle

See photocopiable page 42.

### Objectives

To discover that the radii of circles are equal.
To investigate combinations of coloured sections making full circles.

### Classroom development

Colour one circle yellow and the surrounding square red. Colour the other circle red and the surrounding square yellow.

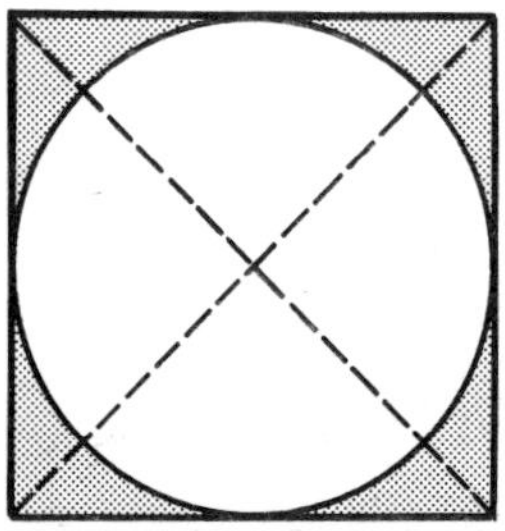

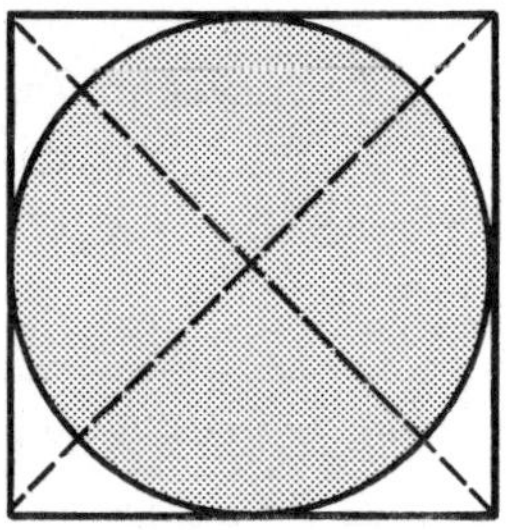

Cut round the outside of the squares. Cut both squares along the dotted lines to make four pieces each. Investigate how many different ways you can combine any four pieces to make circles in squares.

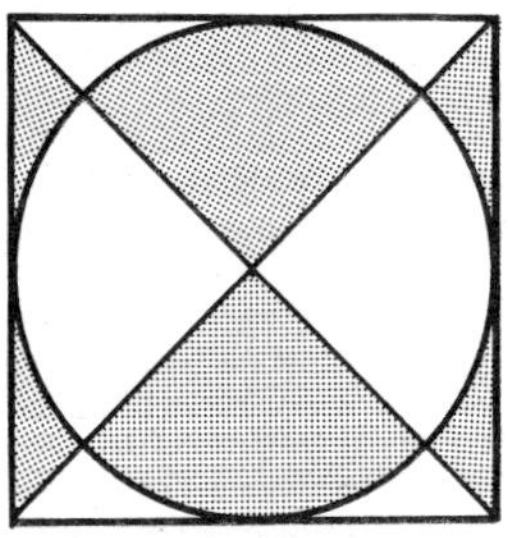

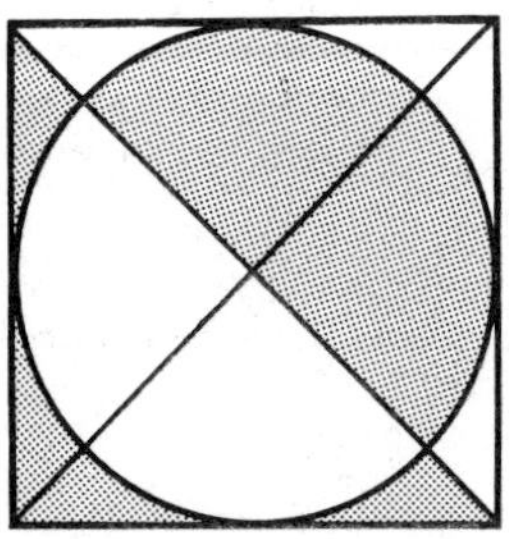

There are six ways in total: two remaking the completely red or yellow circle; two using two pieces from each square and two using three pieces from one square and one piece from another.

### Further activities

Using four colours, colour each quarter of the circles a different colour. Cut out the circles ignoring the square. Cut along the dotted lines. How many different circles can you make? We made 30!

## Spinners

See photocopiable pages 43 and 44.

### Objective

To investigate the rotational symmetry of circles.

### Classroom development

Colour the spinners on page 43 using two colours for each. Cut them out and mount them on to card. Carefully push a cocktail stick through the centre. Spin them and watch the effect.

Repeat the activity using spinner A on page 44. Compare the effect of this spinner with the ones made previously.

Is it possible to make a two-colour pattern on spinner B? Think about how you can do this. Try your method out. What effect do you see now?

Choose your favourite spinner and look at its pattern. Make a spinner of your own using three colours and in a similar pattern to your favourite on the circle marked C. You may like to make another different spinner.

### Further activities

Look at the spinners. Decide which of them would be suitable to mark with numbers for a board game. Make your own simple board game and use your chosen spinner.

# Circle tangram

See photocopiable page 45.

### Objectives

To investigate the properties and line symmetry of circles.

### Classroom development

Cut out the circle and cut along the dotted lines. Remake the circle, can you still see the square? How many different ways can you use the five pieces to make a circle? How many different ways can the square be made?

# Circle patterns

See photocopiable page 46.

### Objectives

To notice circles in patterns, and to create designs from parts of circles.

### Classroom development

Using coloured pens or pencils make an interesting pattern on page 46. Compare it with your friend's pattern. What is the same and what is different about them? Make another different pattern.

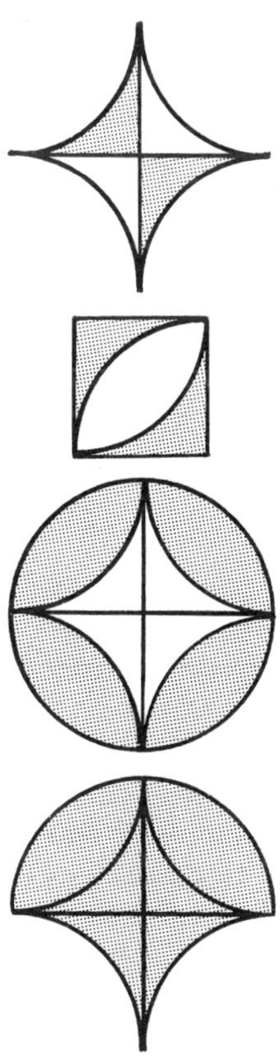

### Further activities

Use the pattern you have made to make some wrapping paper for a gift or to cover a book.

# How many parts?

See photocopiable page 47.

### Objectives

To partition shapes with three straight lines, and to investigate the number of regions created.

### Classroom development

Use three straws to partition the triangles into regions. What is the greatest number of regions you can make? What is the least?

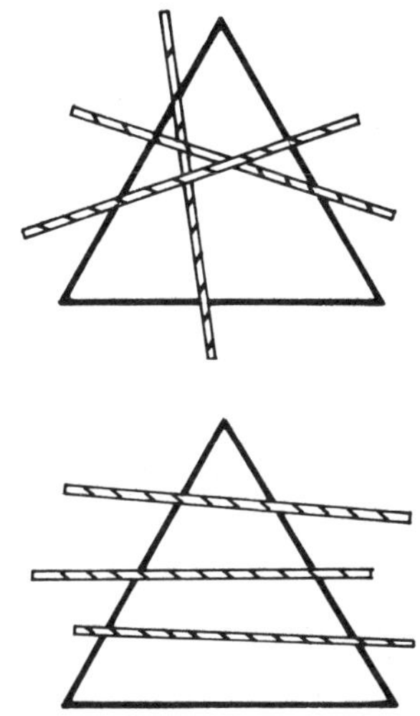

How many different numbers of regions can be made? Record by drawing straight lines on the shapes. Does it matter what shape is used? Try using squares and circles.

Cut out the shapes and sort them according to the number of regions. What do you notice about the lines?

### Further activities

Try this with other shapes or with other numbers of straws such as two or four.

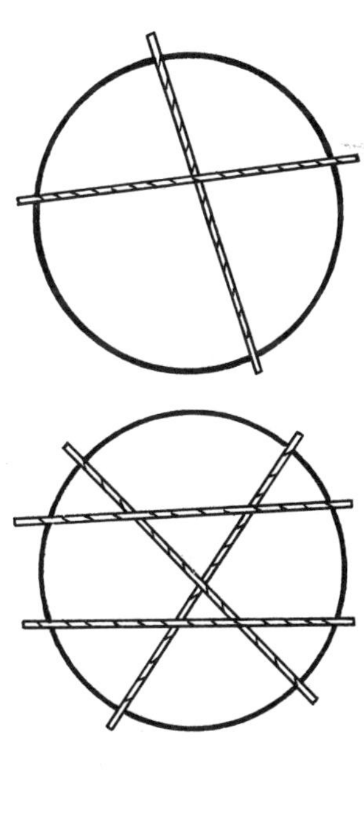

# Square on the circle

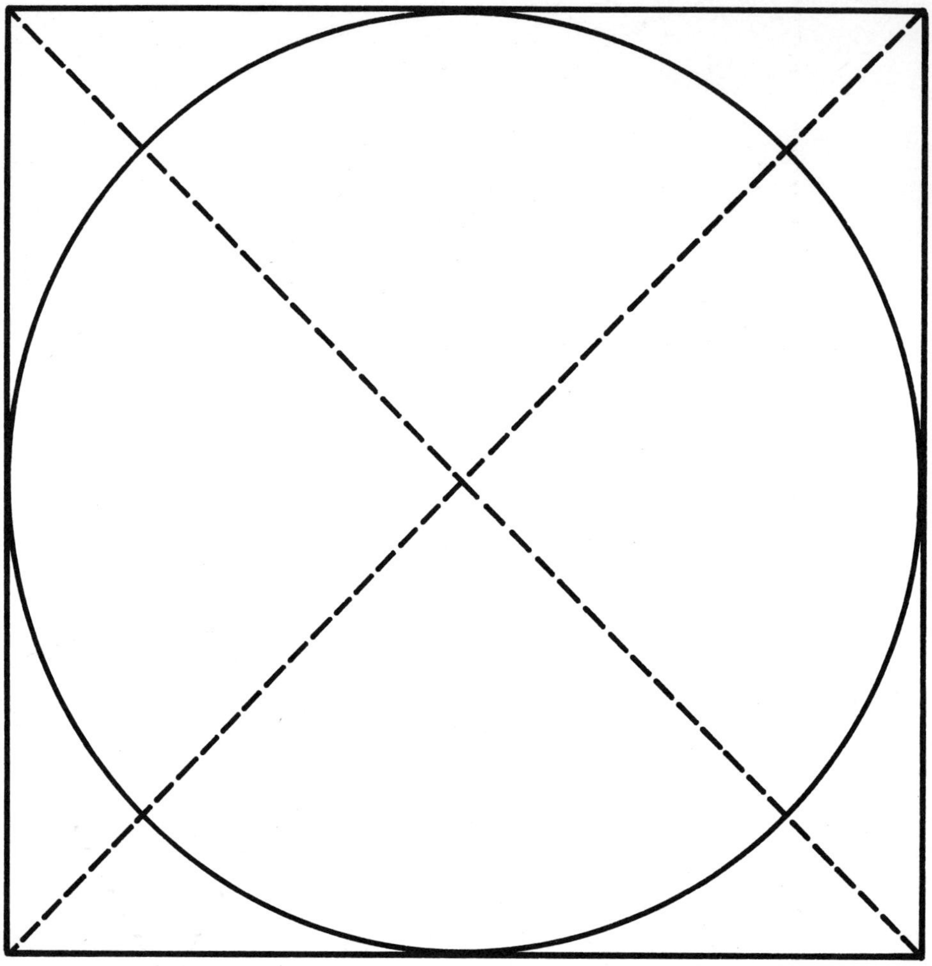

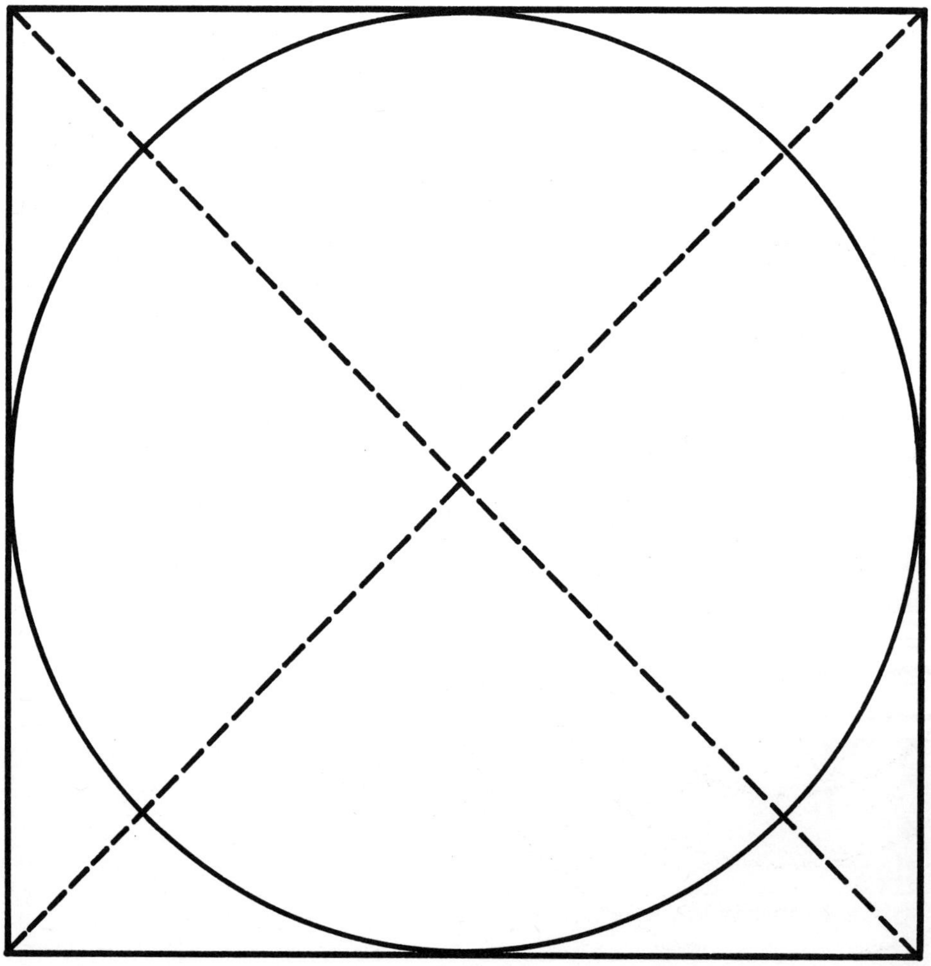

# Spinners

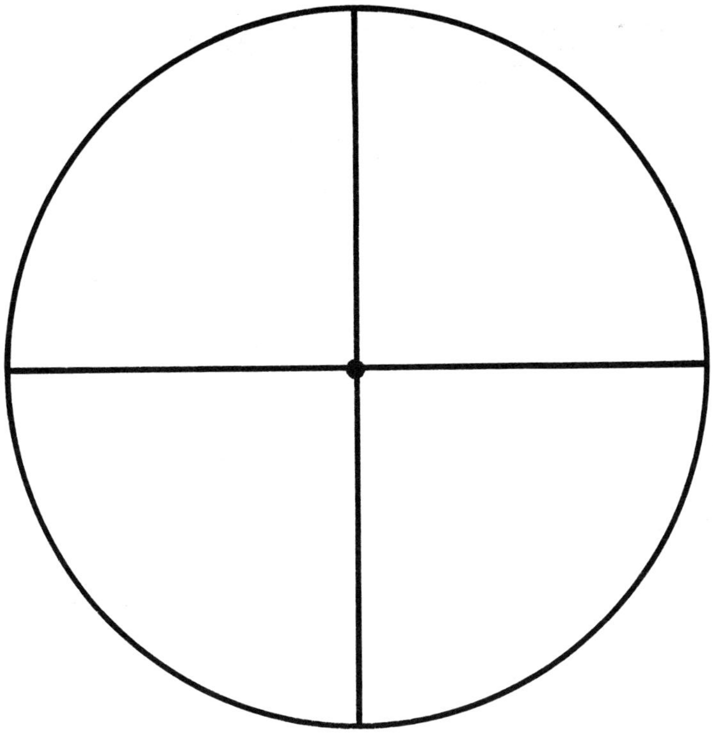

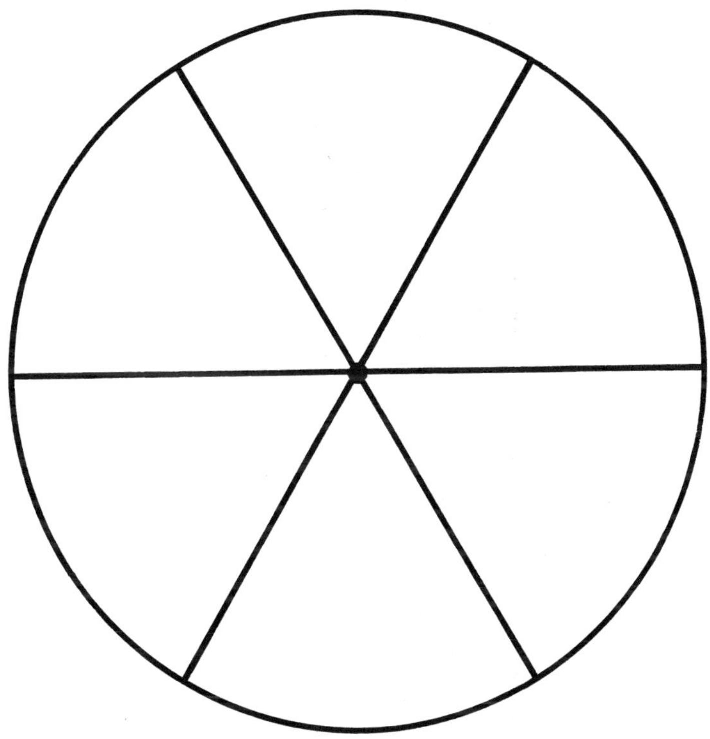

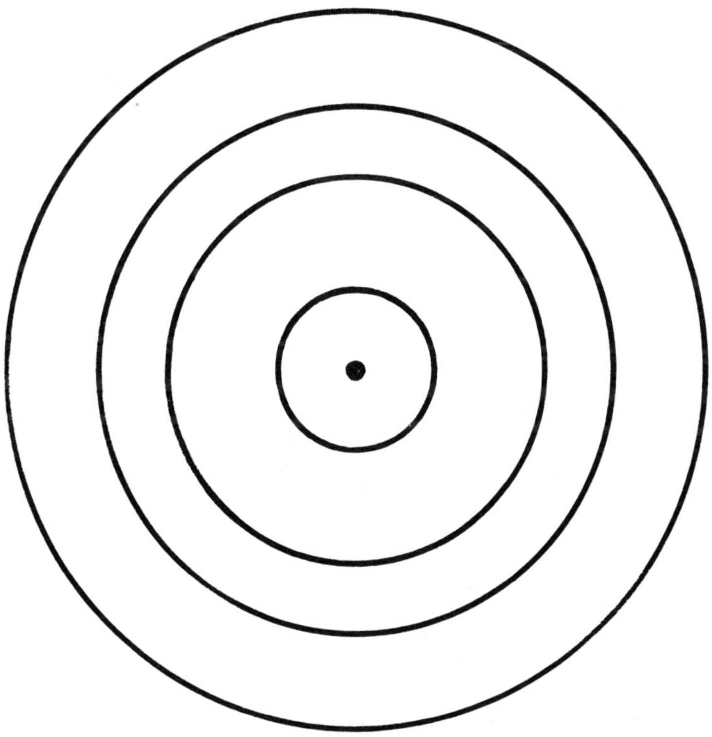

# Spinners

A

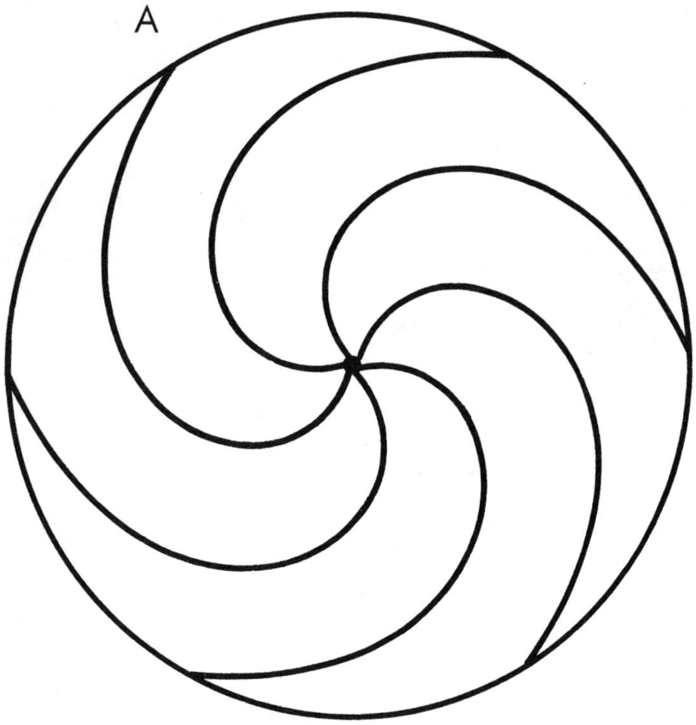

B

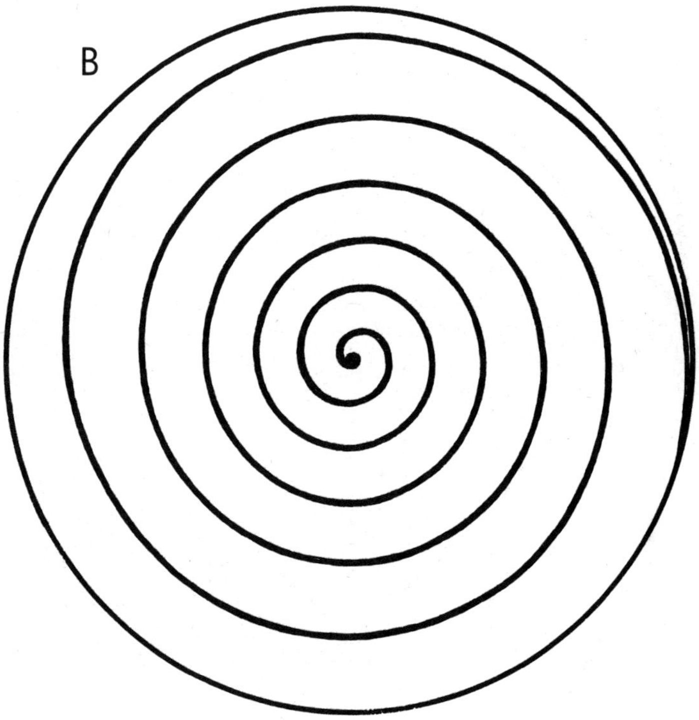

C

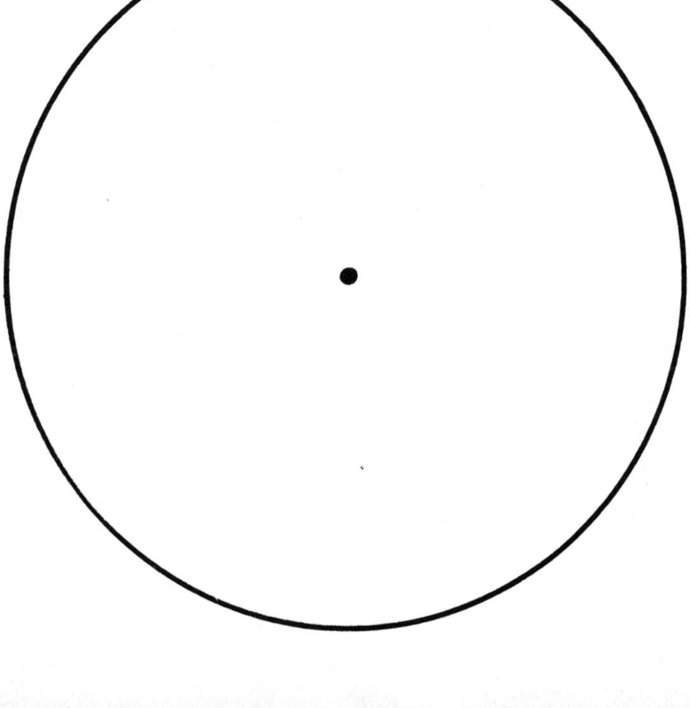

# Circle tangram

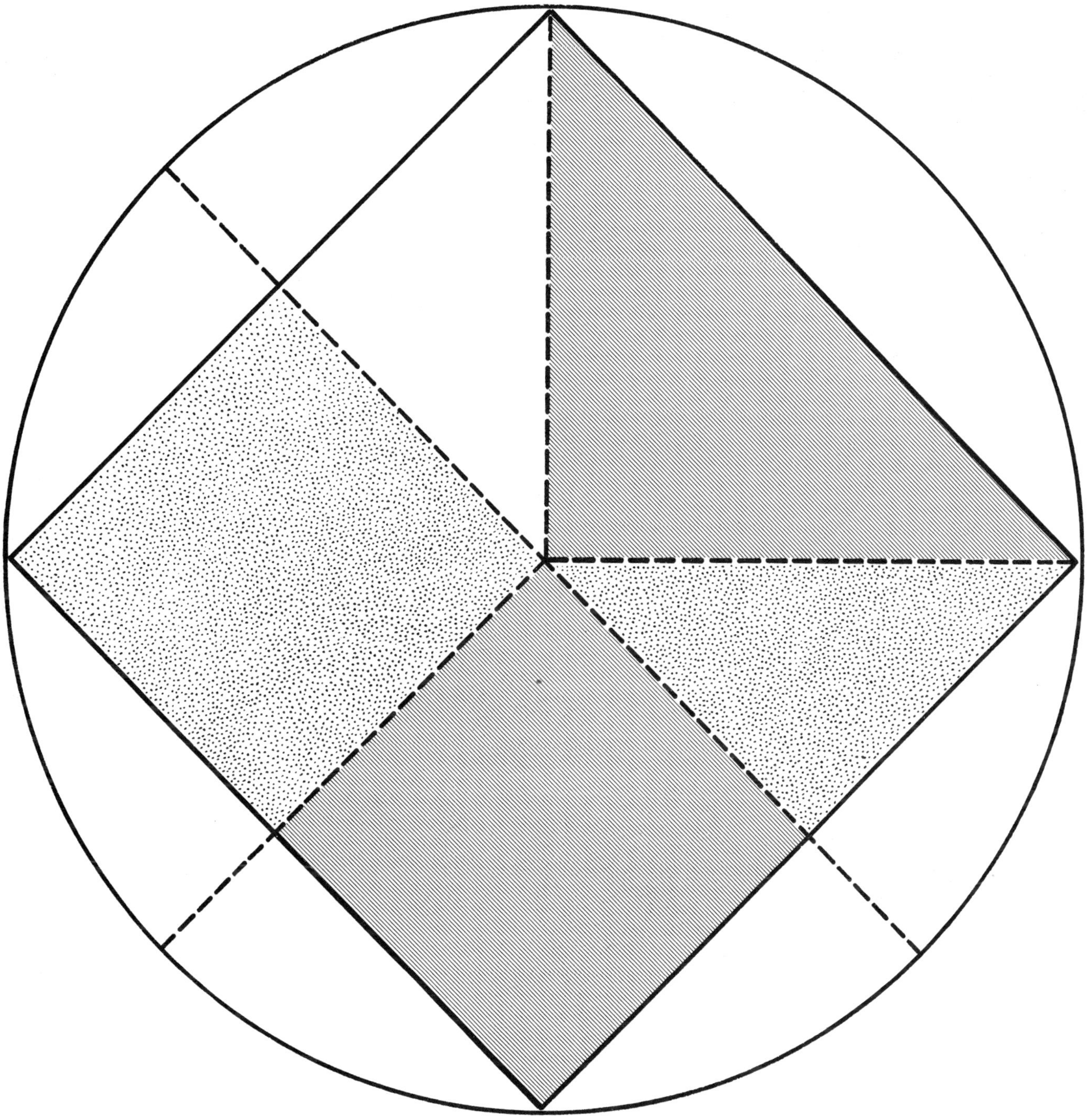

# Circle patterns

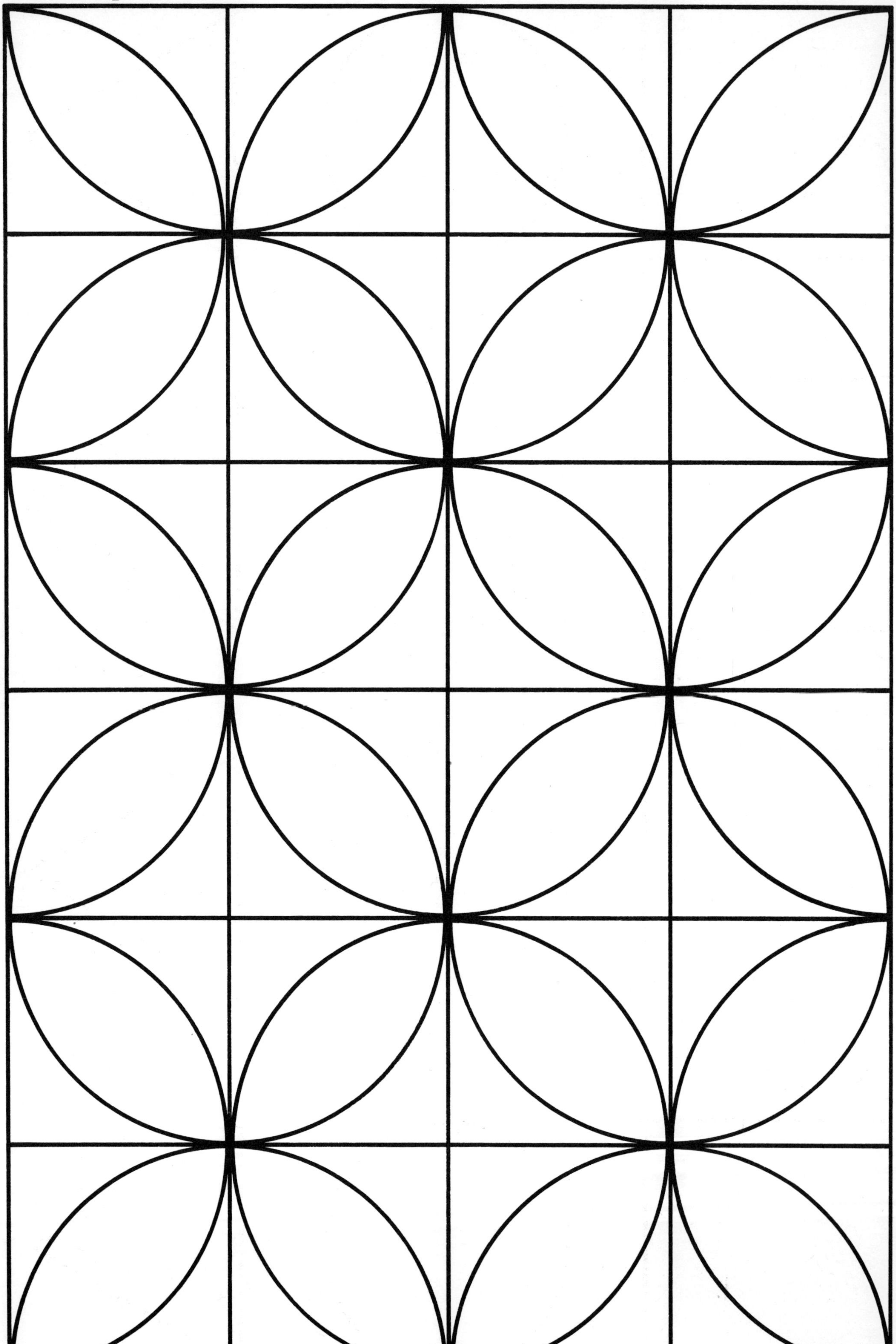

# How many parts?

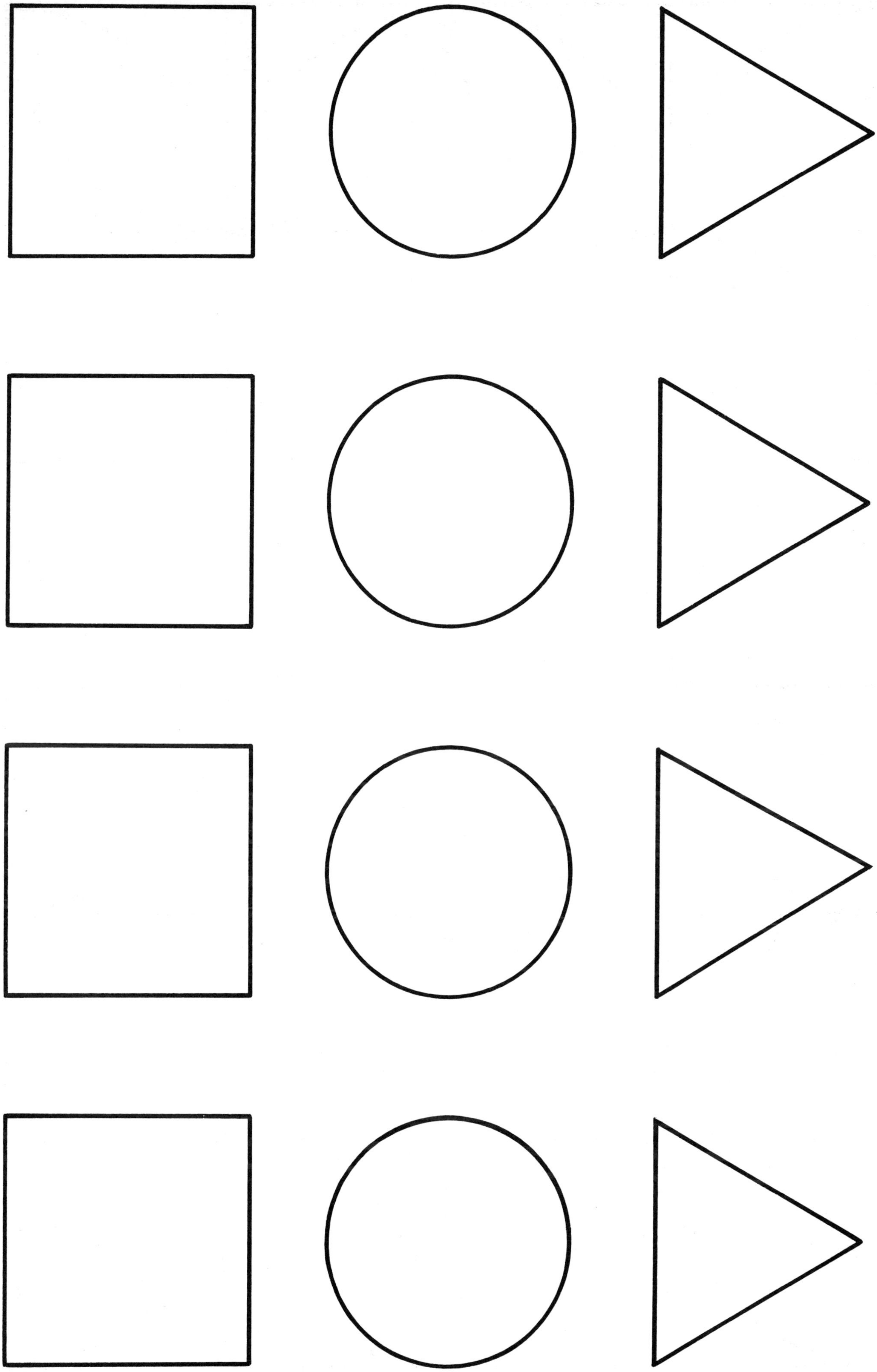

# Other Scholastic books

## Bright Ideas
The *Bright Ideas* books provide a wealth of resources for busy primary school teachers. There are now more than 20 titles published, providing clearly explained and illustrated ideas on topics ranging from *Writing* and *Maths Activities* to *Assemblies* and *Christmas Art and Craft*. Each book contains material which can be photocopied for use in the classroom.

## Teacher Handbooks
The *Teacher Handbooks* give an overview of the latest research in primary education, and show how it can be put into practice in the classroom. Covering all the core areas of the curriculum, the *Teacher Handbooks* are indispensable to the new teacher as a source of information and useful to the experienced teacher as a quick reference guide.

## Management Books
The *Management Books* are designed to help teachers to organise their time, classroom and teaching more efficiently. The books deal with topical issues, such as *Parents and Schools* and organising and planning *Project Teaching*, and are written by authors with lots of practical advice and experiences to share.

## International Bookshelf
The *International Bookshelf* is a selection of informative educational books available in the UK exclusively through Scholastic. Truly representative of international thinking, these books are classics in their own field.

## Big Books
*Big Books* are poster-sized books, aimed at five- to nine-year-olds, which have been specially designed so that a group of children can share a book with an adult and still have that feeling of togetherness which is so important for early readers who are building up confidence. Included in each pack is a giant-sized book, six smaller books for individual reading and teacher notes.

## Infant Science
*Infant Science*, written by teachers and advisers, introduces scientific concepts in non-fiction, easy-to-understand pupil books. Illustrated in full colour, the first books in the series on *Animals* show many aspects of living things from plants, insects and birds to fish and reptiles. A comprehensive teacher's guide giving practical activities and four A2 posters are also available.